Boardsmanship

The Practical Art of Serving as an Executive Board Member

John A. Hazlett, M.B.A., JD

authorHOUSE®

AuthorHouse™
1663 Liberty Drive
Bloomington, IN 47403
www.authorhouse.com
Phone: 1-800-839-8640

First published by AuthorHouse 4/06/2010

ISBN: 978-1-4490-5814-2 (e)
ISBN: 978-1-4490-5815-9 (sc)

Library of Congress Control Number: 2009913401

Printed in the United States of America
Bloomington, Indiana

This book is printed on acid-free paper.

THIS BOOK IS DEDICATED TO FIRST PREBYTERIAN CHURCH, WHEELING, AND ALL THOSE PRESBYTERIANS WHO PRACTICE THEIR FAITH THROUGH WORKS

SPECIAL ACKNOWLEDGEMENT TO DR. WILLIAM E. DEIBERT, WILBUR S. JONES, AND REVEREND J. ROBERT WILLITS FOR THEIR LEADERSHIP AND SUPPORT, AND DR. H. LAWRENCE JONES, WHO IN ADDITION PROVIDED HIS SERVICES AS A FREQUENT SEMINAR LEADER AND INVALUABLE SOUNDING BOARD

FOREWORD

For-profit organizations (fpos) and non-profit organizations (npos) form a significant part of community life and the economy in the United States. The variety of their purposes and sizes presents challenges of analysis, understanding, and efficient and effective operation. The responsibilities of the governing bodies – the boards – of both fpos and npos are essentially the same. The impact of the non-profit sector, however, is less clearly understood.

In the State of West Virginia, for example, there are approximately 10,000 active stand alone npos with another 3,000+ faith based organizations. These organizations together employ upwards of 10% of the State's work force with an impact on the wage base and economy in the hundreds of millions of dollars annually. The number and distribution of npos in West Virginia appears to be representative of the country at large, with the number of people per npo in WV in the general range across all the states.

Governance of these npos would not be possible without the volunteers who serve on their boards in a constant give-and-take of egos, ideas, and responsibilities. Good people with good intentions, who too often do not know enough to know they don't know enough, these board members are under increasing pressure as scrutiny of organization governance practices trickles down from the Federal level to our states and communities, regulation inevitably grows, and the need to know more for effective and efficient governance increases.

This book is designed to act as a practical introduction to what board members do and what they have to know for good governance in both the for-profit and non-profit worlds. Working tools and examples of best practices are presented for use as appropriate. By clarifying the practical and legal expectations of board members, and encouraging pertinent education, the intent is to help board members move from wondering what they are supposed to know and do to how to apply that knowledge to any particular organization.

Here is a thought-provoking synopsis of board member responsibilities and tools to carry out those responsibilities. Just as one size doesn't fit all, no one tool or practice will be best for all fpos or npos. Combining the best practice ideas presented in this synopsis with the particular policies and practices of an organization will enable that organization to build a living reference guide and governance manual that should answer the questions "What do I need to do?" and "What do I need to know?" for any board member on an ongoing basis.

Contents

INTRODUCTION

BOARDSMANSHIP is the term we use to talk about the practical art of serving as an executive board member. Both for-profit organizations and non-profit organizations use boards comprised of individuals who have the legal and moral responsibility to lead the organizations. These groups of individuals, whether in the for-profit world or in the non-profit world, have core responsibilities which can be grouped and analyzed in a number of ways. No matter how they are grouped, however, these responsibilities are basically the same in both the for-profit and non-profit worlds. This resource follows the precedent of dividing the responsibilities into six categories. These categories do not vary between for-profit and non-profit although the emphases will vary. The emphases also will vary from organization to organization in both worlds.

Responsibility for the CEO, for strategic planning for the organization, for obtaining resources for the organization, for monitoring the organization's operations, for the way the organization behaves, and for its own governance are the main categories of obligation for the executive board. All other responsibilities can be listed under one or another of these headings. This discussion reviews each of these areas with an eye to the general circumstances found under each area. Best practices of how different organizations approach different responsibilities are presented. Ideas and opportunities arise out of differences.

BOARDSMANSHIP has been presented in seminar form to a variety of organizations, in both the for-profit and non-profit arenas. Differences of presentation take place to make the topic relevant to the specific audience: for-profits are generally more interested in monitoring operations, whereas non-profits focus more on mission. The essence, nonetheless, is the same.

Participants in the seminars have numbered upwards of 2,000 individuals representing over 200 organizations throughout the State of West Virginia. Some seventy seminars have been held since 2001 with volunteer leaders, including West Virginia Secretary of State Betty Ireland and the author. Learnings from these seminars have been incorporated into subsequent presentations and this book.

CEO

Hire & Fire

Monitor Performance

Mentor

Be A Resource

CEO

The CEO is both a position and a person. The board is responsible for both the position and the person filling that position. In smaller organizations, the board itself may perform some of the usual functions of a CEO, often making administrative decisions as well as filling an advisory and leadership role. Responsibilities may be assigned to an executive committee or individual officers of the board. Where no full-time staff have existed, growth may cause transition to the paid CEO and staff, creating a period of challenge to clearly designate and exercise changing responsibilities.

Where there is flexibility and more than one possible scenario, it is crucial that the different expectations and roles of the board and CEO in regard to administrative matters be clearly set out in job descriptions and written records. Where a term such as Head of Staff is used, it must be clearly defined and the variables in that typical responsibility- such as authority to hire and fire other professional staff, determine staff job descriptions, and obligation to keep and maintain appropriate personnel records- be identified as lying with the CEO or remaining with the board. The CEO's job description and any written contract are usual places to record such definitions. Board minutes may record any understandings not clearly set out elsewhere.

Normal board responsibilities in regard to the CEO can be broken down as follows:

HIRE/FIRE This is really two different processes in most organizations. Most non-profits do not terminate CEOs as well as they hire them. Consequently, termination is often disruptive to the organization and can cause loss of resources to the organization in terms of members and other volunteers who disassociate themselves. It is important to keep all responsible bodies as informed as possible about pertinent information in regard to the CEO.

Hiring of the CEO is a process that varies with the organization. Some local units of national organizations- such as the YWCA- have the responsibility to hire the CEO in the local unit. Other national organizations- such as the Salvation Army-hire the local CEO on a national level and assign the CEO to the local unit. Some organizations have standing committees that carry out hiring; others create ad hoc committees which may include non-board members. Both hiring and firing occur infrequently enough in non-profit organizations that they do not follow the same cycle as membership on the governing board follows. Consequently, whenever these crucial events take place in the life of the organization there often is no one on the board who has been through the process before (national averages for length of service on non-profit boards is between two to three years). Without detailed written record in the organization and established well understood procedures, such event can be traumatic in the life of the organization.

MONITOR PERFORMANCE The governing board has the responsibility to measure the performance of the CEO. In order to do this properly, clear expectations must be set out in job descriptions and contracts. Regular reporting must take place of expected activities and a regular annual review process must be established with the CEO as with other staff. It is the board's responsibility to set up this process. Expectations about the review process itself should be clearly discussed with candidates for all organization positions before hiring, including the CEO. It is a serious mistake to <u>begin</u> a process of CEO evaluation in the midst of conflict.

MENTOR THE CEO It is easy to forget that a CEO has human crises and triumphs that need to be shared and mitigated. It is the board's responsibility to assure that the CEO is not only given the tools necessary to carry out assigned functions, but also receives the personal support to resolve personal issues that can be shared and the educational and other career enhancing support that offer growth in the life of both the CEO and the organization. Usually in a non-profit organization the Chairman of the Board has as one responsibility the coordination of needed care for the CEO. In smaller organizations, the responsibility is more one shared by the whole board, although initiative may be taken by a person or persons on the board with whom the CEO feels comfortable.

BE A RESOURCE The board is the key resource for the CEO. The members are the initial contacts in a network of people resources that, if pursued far enough, can find someone to assist in any situation. The organization as a network begins with the board; networking is the established process to resolving most issues that come before the organization. See "Observations" in the chapter on Resources.

The board itself is also the CEO's prime resource, not only in its skills held by each individual, but also in its knowledge of the organization and its stakeholders, often key to a CEO's success. The board may also act as a resource to other staff members, as staff members may to the board and its committees. This is an area of great potential confusion in the rights and responsibilities of running the organization and expectations must be carefully spelled out.

OBSERVATIONS

- The following section contains examples of documentation used by some organizations.

- It is unfair and chaos-creating to hire a CEO to administer programs and then judge him/her on fund-raising results, and vice – versa. It should be expected that a CEO's duties will be adjusted periodically, including changing emphasis or mix between program administration and fund raising. Such adjustments should be done through a clearly defined process.

- Written employment contracts, reviews, etc. are highly recommended. Minutes should be kept of all meetings and agreed to by all participants. This practice is essential to avoid unnecessary problems with key personnel.

- Most nonprofits are small organizations in which the CEO is responsible for keeping personnel records. Too often this fact means that the CEO keeps his/her own personnel file or has access to it. The CEO's personnel file should be kept by the Chair of the Personnel Committee or other appropriate Board member, with clear succession responsibility. Alternatively, the attorney for the organization is a suitable custodian for the CEO personnel file.

- Understanding the organization's hiring and firing processes should be undertaken by all board members when there is no crisis in the organization. Detailing these processes to the Board, in the absence of other initiative, should be undertaken by the CEO.

- One of the hardest undertakings for any CEO is to plan for his/her successor. The Board should be sure this is an appropriate goal for the CEO and evaluate the CEO on progress towards this goal as towards other goals.

- Many new board members are unsure about staff hiring responsibilities. Usual practice is for the Board to hire the CEO and the CEO to hire other staff to fill positions which have been defined and approved by the Board. Key hirings may require approval of the Board. Performance results of staff hirings are a valid criterion for evaluating the CEO.

- Small organizations often do not offer clear career paths for their CEOs. Whether it is through continued education, participation in a national association, or other creative avenue, it is the Board's responsibility to develop a career path for the CEO. If the position is a dead end, then sooner or later a "dead end" will end up in the position and that is likely to be a dead end for the organization.

CEO JOB DESCRIPTION

❖ Maintain a clear mission statement and strategic plan

❖ Maintain an active Board that provides good governance

❖ Manage programs and services to carry out the organization mission

❖ Be Head of Staff

❖ Develop and manage realistic budgets

❖ Obtain and sustain operating funds and long-term financial resources

❖ Recruit and manage volunteers

❖ Maintain professional surroundings and safe working environment

❖ Report regularly to stakeholders, including public

Note: Responsibilities may be prioritized or emphasized for expansion as opposed to maintenance; annual changes in priorities and expansion versus maintenance are appropriate; specific goals should be set annually in each of these areas. Where needed, definitions of detail may be added (e.g. "Head of Staff" as attached). Clarity may also call for commentary such as "under the policies and decisions established by the Board" or "in accordance with the directions of the Board".

CEO MONITORING

Keeping track of and reviewing the activities of a CEO is a challenge. There are two main reasons to do it. First, it is a good way for a CEO to organize himself or herself and to self-adjust activities as needed to meet the mission of the organization. Second, it is the base for information the board needs to adjust the goals and activities of the CEO in a formal manner in job descriptions and annual reviews and goal settings. This review may be separate from how the CEO has carried out the job; but without this basic information the board has no objective information on how the CEO's activities relate to the organization's effectiveness in carrying out its mission. Reported results are just that-results; they do not tell the board whether a particular activity is necessary to or effective in reaching those results. Conversely, of course, absence of a particular activity may explain absence of a particular result; or reporting of an activity expected to reach a result that does not happen may point to futility of that activity because of either obscure barriers or wrong assumptions. This critical piece of the monitoring process: the log, or activities report; that every npo CEO should keep is usually something that an npo CEO has not kept in the past. Implementing the CEO's keeping of a log, therefore, is often the most difficult part of the monitoring process.

Nonprofits are generally in the service business. CEOs of nonprofits, to provide the best service to stakeholders, often cannot keep regular "business" hours. One effective means of measuring a CEO's time commitment is to divide the week into "modules", with a module usually being defined as a three-hour consecutive time commitment. The expected time for a CEO to spend each week, then, can be defined in "modules", which can be morning, afternoon, or evening. A 36 hour week can then be determined to be 12 modules, with actual time spent varying week to week according to the demands the CEO needs to meet. At the CEO's discretion, spending these modules at different times in different weeks makes it all the more difficult for a board that meets monthly to have a true picture of the time involvement of a CEO position. Many organizations which keep track of modules expect their CEOs to spend a minimum of 14 to 15 modules a week. The accompanying CEO ACTIVITIES REPORT is but one example of how such tracking can be kept. Note that it ties to the CEO JOB DESCRIPTION also enclosed as an example.

CEO ACTIVITIES REPORT period _____ to _____

Activity	Quantity	Hours Spent (approx)
Planning		
Stakeholder consultations		
Planning meetings		
Goal review/results measurement		
Maintain an active Board		
Meetings with Chair/ individual members		
Committee meetings		
Report preparation and delivery		
Manage programs and services		
Staff meetings		
Other stakeholder meetings		
General administration		
Head of Staff		
Resource to staff		
Maintain personnel records		
Schedule work, including vacations		
Develop and manage budgets		

Expenditures review, approval		
Financial report preparation, review		
Audit		
Financial resources/ obtain & sustain		
Donor identification/ solicitation		
Fund-raising activities		
Grant seeking		
Recruit and manage volunteers		
Identification/solicitation		
Match with programs		
Recognition		
Maintain professional, safe work environment		
Risk management		
Culture control		
Education		
Report regularly to stakeholders		
Governing bodies reporting		
Public reporting		
Other stakeholder reporting		

HEAD OF STAFF

SUPERVISE DIRECT REPORTING PERSONNEL

Schedule work, including vacations
Serve as initial grievance channel
Implement Board decisions
Participate in annual staff review

REPORT REGULARLY TO BOARD ABOUT STAFF

Serve on Personnel Committee (hire, fire recommendations originate here)
Recommend position, job descriptions changes, etc.
Recommend staff measurement and evaluation methods
Recommend disciplinary actions

ACT AS RESOURCE TO STAFF

Teach and communicate as appropriate
Source needed training
Access resources needed to carry out jobs efficiently and effectively

MAINTAIN PERSONNEL RECORDS IN SAFETY AND CONFIDENCE

ENSURE SAFE, COMFORTABLE WORK ENVIRONMENT

STRATEGIC PLANNING

VISION

MISSION

VALUES

PROCESS

STRATEGIC PLANNING

Strategic planning is a process that is as essential to a non-profit entity as it is to a for-profit corporation. Long-term viability of any organization is dependent on its continuing to use its resources in the best manner in its environment to accomplish the organization's purposes. Periodic revisiting of these purposes and plans to carry them out not only keeps an organization aware of changes it must make to meet changes in its environment, but also keeps key constituencies of the organization- its "stakeholders"- involved in the organization's purposes and future. The following discussion focuses on four aspects of strategic planning.

VISION Many non-profits do not have a written vision statement. Creating one is very important; revisiting an existing statement every three to five years also is very important. The importance lies as much in the process as the result, because the process will bring to light differences of opinion and expectations in the stakeholders and, if done properly, will reconcile those opinions and expectations into a mutually perceived future. Lack of this periodically verified mutual perception will, over time, lead to conflicts.

A Vision Statement has been defined variously. One definition is "a written statement of what the organization should look like in a certain number of years". Some of the characteristics of such a statement have been put forth as realism, idealism, inspiration, clarity, challenge and attainability. Others view the Vision Statement as the destiny, the ultimate goal that the organization strives to achieve. Whatever words are used, it is the ideal state of the organization in a real world, alive to its environment. Like an ideal marriage, its nuances may change with experience and it may never be quite achieved, and some will come a lot closer than others, but it is in the reaching for it that vitality and growth are nourished.

MISSION More organizations have mission statements than vision statements, but again the periodic review is often neglected. Like with the vision statement, the benefit is as much in the process as the result and revisiting it should be formally on the schedule of an organization's activities. Causing this to happen is a board responsibility.

If the vision is considered the destiny, the mission may be referred to as the journey. It is a written statement of the organization's purpose and prime role. One widely accepted structure of a mission statement is division into three sections: a purpose statement, a business statement, and a values statement. The Mission Statement of First Church Wheeling is enclosed as an example of such a three-part statement.

VALUES All activities of an organization take place in an atmosphere of at least acceptance and often active encouragement of certain kinds of behavior. In for profit organizations this behavior may be called "culture"; this reference is usable for nonprofits as well. It is clear that behavior has impact on all stakeholders of an organization, including the public. Consequently, behavior of an organization should not only be recognized, but also planned for and integrated into the strategic plan as a crucial part of the story for success that is being crafted.

For an individual, it has been said that values lie where the passions of avocation intersect with the path of vocation. It would appear to be the same for an organization-values occur where the fires of purpose connect with the art of the possible; where dreams are interpreted in the context of capacity. Identifying a number of core values for the grounding of this dreaming is an essential part of the planning process.

PROCESS   The process of Strategic Planning can vary, but it has a certain progression that has been developed through experience as effective. This progression includes obtaining the input of stakeholders in the organization. In most non-profits, this includes not only the board and committees, but often also the membership, staff, donors, and volunteers. The process begins with brainstorming ideas and then refining and combining until a focus can be derived. From that focus the Vision and Mission are developed with specific goals and objectives established as steps to carrying out the Mission and achieving the Vision, all in the context of the Values agreed to as the set of assumptions for how the organization will behave.

Planners vary on their use of "goals" and "objectives", making distinctions between characteristics of time horizons, specificity, and hierarchical position. Traditional professional management teaching equates "goals" and "objectives". It is not important what phraseology is used so long as the definitions are clear and use is consistent. This discussion uses "goals", which for these purposes may also be read as "objectives". Goals are achievable, measurable acts that are to be completed within a defined time frame. Some planning puts goals out no longer than two to three years-others distinguish between short-term goals (less than one year out) and long-term (one to three years out). In strategic planning, setting goals to accomplish the mission-and ultimately the vision- is a necessary next step to making the mission and vision happen. Goals themselves need to be prioritized and work plans developed to reach them.

In most organizations the usual methodology for this next step is the assignment to pertinent committees the responsibility for developing work plans and procedures to recommend to the board to reach different goals. In organizations with large paid staffs, the responsibility may be assigned to them. The board should approve and change these recommendations as necessary. The responsibility to carry out these plans and procedures may be assigned back to the originating committee, another committee or task force, or to the CEO and staff. The board must allocate the necessary resources to carry out these work plans; and the responsibility to monitor progress and measure results.

It is extremely important in a formal strategic planning process to be led by an outsider to the organization. Not only does an outsider bring necessary objectivity to the process, but also an expertise in conducting the process that is usually not available inside the organization. When the expertise is available inside the organization, using that expertise excludes those people from participating in the opinion rendering and discussion that they are entitled to as part of the organization.

OBSERVATIONS

- The following pages give an example of a Mission Statement and elaborate on values and a possible outline for a process.

- The most important part of any Strategic Planning process is getting the right participation. The Board must carefully include the right groups and must be sure that the individuals participating are given full opportunity for input, as ownership in the process is crucial for ownership in the outcome. Even if differences of opinion are evident, opportunity to express and defend those differences is essential for cooperation in any compromise result. As purportedly stated by one of our native West Virginians "if I'm not in on it or up on it, I'm down on it". It is human nature.

- Clearly, an experienced moderator must run any effective strategic planning process. Equally important, enough time must be allocated to carry out the process properly. Two or three hours will not do a comprehensive job.

- Where there is potential for different interpretations, clarity of definitions should be the first order of business. What scope of the organization's activities is the topic – i.e. the whole organization, or just a component of it – affects the discussion. For example, at one level there should be no argument that an individual public elementary school should have the same mission as the whole county school system. At another level, the implementation may be different and require "tactical" as opposed to "strategic" thinking. Number of years planned for and frequency of the planning will affect the thinking. Mutual understanding of the planning parameters of these and other factors is essential for an effective process.

- Any planning process that does not include the "allocators" of organization resources as an integral part from the beginning is broken. By "allocators" I mean those with the right and responsibility to determine how all of the organization's resources are to be employed – and developed.

FIRST PRESBYTERIAN CHURCH

WHEELING, WEST VIRGINIA

MISSION STATEMENT

We are a congregation gathered to live the ministry of the one Word of God and to glorify our Lord by developing Christian disciples.

We are a community of rich heritage with an urban center of hope, home, and wholeness providing Christian nurture, worship, prayer, Bible study, fellowship, and service.

We are a family that values and fosters change, inclusiveness, acceptance, responsibility, learning, empowerment, and trust.

VALUES

Values should be considered in regard to the different functions and stakeholders of the organization. There are certain management values – such as accuracy, promptness, and courtesy – which can be readily understood and accepted and may be considered such a part of our national culture that they don't need to be singled out and detailed as to what is acceptable and what is not. Each organization may be content to simply recite those they expect and detail them further if necessary.

Other values – such as confidentiality and community focus – may require detailing as to what is expected in terms of different stakeholders in the organization. For example, what is confidential treatment of employees may differ from what is confidential treatment of donors both legally and practically.

If one of the values of the organization is community focus, this may mean that the organization looks first – or only – to community members for its hires, offers its services only to community members, but may solicit beyond community members to provide resources to the organization.

In defining an npo's mission, it makes sense to focus on those values which distinguish it from the general population of non-profit organizations: such as "client run", "no fee for services", "senior citizen focus", "24 – 7 service", "enhancing wildlife habitat", etc.. In other words, focus on what sets your organization apart from others.

PROCESS

1. Revisit the Vision Statement

2. Affirm the Values of the organization.

3. Revisit the Mission Statement. One approach is to develop the Mission Statement as a 1) Purpose Statement, 2) Business Statement, and 3) Value Statement. The First Church Mission Statement may be broken down in this fashion. Others believe a Mission Statement should be no more than six to ten words long. The ideal format should be agreed to early.

4. Do a S.W.O.T. analysis.

  i.   Strengths   (internal)
  ii. Weaknesses   (internal
  iii. Opportunities (external)
  iv. Threats   (external)

5. Develop S.M.A.R.T. goals.

  i.   S: specific
  ii. M: measurable
  iii. A: achievable
  iv. R: realistic
  v.   T: time-defined

6. Develop a work plan to reach the goals.

7. Ask the appropriate body (the Board?) to allocate the resources necessary to carry out the work plan.

8. Oversee the work plan (usually the CEO and Board Committee Chairs).

9. Report and react at regular Board meetings.

10. Those goals not reached according to plan should be re-evaluated for inclusion in the next plan.

RESOURCES

PEOPLE

FACILITIES

FUNDS

COLLABORATORS

BOARD

RESOURCES

Traditionally resources are discussed in terms of three categories: people, facilities, and funds. This summary highlights, in addition, other organizations in a category called "collaborators" and the board itself for a total of five topical areas.

Obtaining resources is a three step process: identifying, recruiting, and institutionalizing (making a permanent part of the organization). This process has a cost to the organization in each step; and each step probably varies from resource to resource as well as organization to organization. How well an organization performs each of these steps also will vary from resource to resource and organization to organization. Nonetheless, there are general statements which may be made about each category which can serve as overall guides to better resource origination and utilization.

PEOPLE Every organization's most important resource is people. A useful way to think about people as a resource is to break them down into types.

PROFESSIONAL STAFF: This is all paid employees. Professional staff are found in usual personnel recruitment ways. Professional recruiters, reference from organization regional and national bodies, advertisement, reference from board and other members, and reference from present professional staff are the prime ways. In some organizations, the national parent may choose the local CEO.

All staff must be treated in a professional manner with proper detailed expectations, regular mutual review, and appropriate record keeping. Communication and regular procedures are essential elements for good professional staff origination and retention. Clear understanding of what is expected from any particular position is a necessary prelude to filling that position.

VOLUNTEERS: This term may be applied to all other people involved in an organization. Some organizations do not think of volunteers, but rather members. There is a tendency to think of the two as identical. They are not. Where members form the largest and most available body of people to be volunteers in helping carry out an organization's mission, some of the most effective programs of the organization may be energized and accomplished by volunteers who are not members.

The challenge here is to develop methods to maximize use of volunteers. This challenge takes two paths: member volunteers and non-member volunteers. Knowing more about member volunteers and their respective skills and backgrounds is the first step to greater participation. Conducting a member survey and building a consequent member skills inventory is the traditional way to accomplish this first step. Asking members to volunteer is the second step. Some organizations ask members to enlist in specific areas of participation in a printed form that details these areas. This form may be distributed annually. The areas on the form may, of course, be changed periodically.

The most practical way to enlist aid of non-member volunteers in organization activities is through specific programs. Specific programs often carry interest for others who are not members but are looking for opportunities to serve. Volunteers who come to the organization for participation in programs offer an obvious potential source of future organization members.

Crucial for successful finding and keeping of volunteers for organizations is to assign responsibility for doing that to established, regular parts of the organizations. Effective use of volunteers takes a clear, regular application of these responsibilities by an effective body in the governance structure. In non-profit organizations, this responsibility usually falls ultimately on the CEO. Where there is no clear pattern of non-member volunteer responsibility, this is an area for major potential development.

MEMBERS (OWNERS): In the for-profit world, these would be shareholders. In non-profit organizations, these are the people who pay dues and fulfill the other functions required of members. In one way or another, they are the people who ultimately determine the future of the organization to which they belong. They do not have day-to-day governance responsibilities, but they usually ultimately determine who does have those responsibilities and therefore the direction the organization will take. Often they have specific rights to vote on key issues facing the organization.

Members' most effective influence is often informal and the challenge for the board is to communicate with them regularly and effectively. Some established methods of communicating include periodic information meetings, publication of board minutes, and regular newsletters. Information posted on organization premises is also important. Two way communication is essential. The method with most potential for the future- the internet- is often underdeveloped in the individual organization.

A significant factor in working with some non-profit organizations' members is to understand that in many respects the members, in addition to being volunteers, may be the prime clients of the organization.

CLIENTS (Customers): These are the people who are the recipients of the organization's services. Obviously, the for-profit community calls them customers and sometimes clients as well. One major distinction is that for-profit clients pay for services. Non-profit clients, if they pay at all, pay a reduced rate.

Clear understanding of the priority of members as clients for an organization's services and outreach is important to an organization's viability.

OTHERS: This catchall category of people includes everyone else who might come into contact with the organization. Main groups would include donors, family and friends, and often public figures such as local politicians and business leaders. CEOs of other non-profits could be considered here as well.

FACILITIES   An obvious resource, physical plant forms a focus for any non-profit. It is a center for activities that becomes a community identification for the organization. Although it does not deliver services by itself, it becomes a mechanism for evoking positive feelings about those services. As memories around a building accumulate, the power of that evocation in non-members as well as clients and members grows as well. Use of buildings is an important part of that memory creation.

Programming which cannot be housed in the organization's own facilities may be able to be housed in other facilities. Often communities have community facilities that may be used by groups in the community. Other non-profits, including churches, frequently have areas that can be used by medium to large groups. Businesses too, such as banks, will make facilities available for certain events. The challenge for the board is to organize the finding of these needed facilities. Personal contacts of board members are often key.

FUNDS Funding for non-profit organizations is usually analyzed as falling into three types determined by their purposes. Raising these funds is dependent on the type and professional fund-raising has become a recognized expertise marketed by specialists around the country. Often these specialists may be found in the local organization's national affiliate.

OPERATING: As the title indicates, these are monies used to pay daily operating expenses. Annual pledge drives and special events are traditional ways to raise these funds. Some organizations supplement these sources with income from endowments. Different organizations use different events and program methodologies to raise these monies. Surveys of regional and national experiences in these areas should give any local organization good ideas. Again, there is the challenge of centralizing responsibility for carrying out these efforts in the governance structure.

BUILDING: Limited to campaigns for remodeling existing structures, building new structures, acquiring needed structures and certain high-cost equipment, raising these funds is a special case. Usually viewed as one-time gifts, requests for help in these matters have a different character. Naming for a prominent donor, linking to certain investment and tax advantages, and opening up new potential donor classes such as local corporations distinguish this type of fund-raising from operating fund solicitation. Special funds for these purposes, not available for operating funds, may exist at an organization's regional and national affiliates. Some foundations may assist these types of projects. Each potential source carries particular details and requirements.

ENDOWMENT: Also referred to as permanent funds, these are monies that are usually obtained by bequests from members- and non-members. Like the other two main types of funds, these must be found by dedicated effort on the part of a responsible body in the governance of the organization. This effort is long-term and often does not bear fruit for years. The fruit, however, may continue to bear from well-done efforts for a long time. Special purpose funds as well as general benefit funds can be raised through this type of campaign. Expertise in this area may be available through an organization's national affiliate as well as through independent fund-raisers.

COLLABORATORS A term which has grown up in the last decade or so, it is used to refer to other organizations which may work with a particular organization to accomplish limited programs or long-term joint purpose activities. Government organizations as well as private corporations, non-profit organizations with similar particular interests but no formal affiliation, and affiliated organizations all can be collaborators. In the private sector these relationships are usually referred to as partnerships or joint ventures; such partnerships are usually characterized by more formal legal agreements and have longer life spans than collaborative arrangements. In the private sector there is also a question of residual "ownership" value, which usually does not play a significant role in collaborative relationships.

BOARD As a group of individuals bringing various experiences to the organization, the board itself offers an often under-utilized resource. Requirements as to qualification for sitting on the board do not bring individual backgrounds, skills, and interests necessarily to light. There is only one way to do that-ask. Obtaining detailed knowledge of board members' experiences and making them available to the board is necessary to maximizing the effectiveness of the organization's governing body. Not only are the individual's personal abilities valuable, but the contacts that individual made during employment or other experience can be crucial to effective and efficient operation of the organization, from checking references to understanding the best way to carry out a repair.

OBSERVATIONS

- Sample documentation used by some organizations is found in this section. You will note that the skills, etc. inventories are relatively complex. Simpler forms may be more appropriate for any individual organization.

- Statistics analyze that more often than not there are only three people between any individual and any other individual in the country who know one another on a first name basis. The challenge is to find the network of those three individuals. Combine this interesting statistic with the empiric realization that there are few challenges or opportunities facing an organization that cannot be solved or pursued by knowing the right person, and the networking capability of an organization becomes the key resource for that organization. The first link in the chain of this network for an organization is the individual board member. Providing the CEO with appropriate information about the board member's background, contacts, etc. becomes crucial for the organization.

- Many board members do not feel comfortable committing to "financially support" the organization, particularly in fund raising. One of the details found here is a break-down of different levels of financial support for an organization showing how a volunteer can effectively provide financial support to an organization without necessarily having to ask others for money.

- Specific professional training for board members on how to ask a potential donor for money can be essential to overcoming psychological barriers as well as providing needed technical knowledge.

BOARD SERVICE SKILLS GRID EXPERIENCE/UNDERSTANDING

	SERVED AS/ON	WORKED WITH	IN THEORY	NO
CEO				
CEO				
BOARD OFFICER				
BOARD MEMBER				
CEO SEARCH COMMITTEE				
CEO EVALUATION COMMITTEE				
HR MANAGEMENT				
STRATEGIC PLANNING				
STAKEHOLDER IN STRATEGIC PLAN DEVELOPMENT				
LEADER IN STRATEGIC PLAN DEVELOPMENT				
FACILITATOR OF STRATEGIC PLAN DEVELOPMENT				
RESOURCES				
PERSONNEL RECRUITING/ EVALUATION				
FINANCIAL MANAGEMENT/ BUDGETING				
FUND-RAISING				
PHYSICAL PLANT MANAGEMENT/ CONSTRUCTION				
COMMUNITY SERVICE				
MONITORING OPERATIONS				
ANALYZING/ UNDERSTANDING FINANCIAL STATEMENTS				
MEASURING RESULTS VS GOALS				
SERVICE BUSINESS MANAGEMENT				

SELF-GOVERNANCE				
ORGANIZATIONAL DEVELOPMENT				
NOMINATING COMMITTEE				
OTHER COMMITTEE(S)				
MANAGING VOLUNTEERS				
LEGAL TRAINING				
BEHAVIOR				
RISK MANAGEMENT				
PUBLIC RELATIONS				
CLIENT SERVICE				

BOARD MEMBER CHARACTERISTICS GRID
EDUCATION/TALENT

	FORMAL TRAINING	EXPER-IENCE	NATIVE ABILITY	AMATEUR INTEREST	AVERAGE PERSON
MUSIC					
SINGING					
PIANO PLAYING					
PLAY INSTRUMENT					
COMPOSITION					
THEATER					
ACTED					
DIRECTED					
SCENERY, PROPS					
WRITER					
"HANDYMAN"					
CARPENTRY					
ELECTRICAL					
PAINTING					
PLUMBING					
DESIGN					
TEACHING					
FORMAL JOB					
TUTOR					
COACH					
YOUTH					
ADULTS					
LANGUAGES					
SPEAK FOREIGN LAN					
WRITE FOREIGN LAN					
OTHER (e.g. SEWING, COOKING,GARDENING)					

BOARD MEMBER CONTACT GRID
PEOPLE/PLACES

	ORGANIZATION	POSITION	TIME SPENT	CURRENT?
WORK				
SCHOOLS				
HOMES				
MEMBERSHIPS				
VOLUNTEER				

OTHER				

LEVELS OF FINANCIAL SUPPORT FOR AN NPO
BOARD MEMBERS & VOLUNTEERS

LEVEL ONE (Board members)

1. Make an annual personal financial contribution.

2. Understand each income source and expense category, the reasons for the levels of each set in the budget, and the timing expected for receipt from each income source and for each expense throughout the budgeted year.

3. Recommend changes in the budget necessary to keep it balanced when there is reasonable belief that any income source or expense category amount projected in the budget becomes significantly inaccurate.

4. Identify potential sources of income and expense mitigation for follow-up by the staff.

LEVEL TWO (Board members and volunteers)

1. Participate directly with an income source or expense generator to verify, and if possible assure, that the budget expectations will be met or improved upon; and, or

2. Participate directly with a specific fund-raising activity to benefit the organization or a specific project to reduce expenses for the organization.

LEVEL THREE (Board members and volunteers)

1. Participate as a planner and support in a focused fund-raising campaign for general operations, a capital project, or a permanent fund development; and, or

2. Participate through personal contact with potential funding sources, individuals and institutions, in a focused fund-raising campaign for general operations, a capital project, or a permanent fund development.

MONITORING OPERATIONS

FINANCIAL REPORTING

NON-FINANCIAL REPORTING

RESOURCE UTILIZATION

PROGRAM REVIEW

MONITORING OPERATIONS

The board has the obligation to monitor operations of the organization; to oversee what the organization is doing, how it is doing it, and why it is doing it. But the obligation does not stop with analysis; the analysis, in order to have meaning, must relate to standards and goals. These are the standards and goals as developed through the strategic planning process. Without the monitoring, feedback, and necessary adjustments along the way by the board, the realities fulfilling dreams may remain ever out of reach. Implementation starts with the board.

Monitoring requires an infrastructure. The systems must exist to gather the necessary information, the people and skills need to be in place to run those systems, and the necessary information must be presented in a timely manner to the board and the organization's leaders to be useful; and the board must have the ability to understand the information. Special knowledge training may be needed. Four major categories and systems used to monitor operations of non-profit organizations are addressed in this section.

FINANCIAL REPORTING Every organization needs to know how it is doing financially. Money, as a resource, is often the tool that makes the other resources effective. Reports to the board on the financial activities should be regular (monthly is recommended), thorough and readily understood. Proper accounting for non-profits differs in some important aspects from for-profit accounting and even experienced business people may need some specialized training in reading complicated non-profit financial reports. In a non-profit where separate funds may be the responsibility of separate individuals and committees, presenting a consolidated picture may be particularly challenging. Often legal restrictions on different bodies of funds are not readily apparent and may require footnoted or other informative addenda.

Many non-profits are required to do an annual financial audit. There are degrees of audit, and the board should keep in mind that varying the methodology from time to time can be both effective and efficient. There may also be questions as to what funds are to be included in the audit. What information- audit or other-should be provided to various stakeholders in the organization, as well as what may be required to be provided, is up to the board.

NON-FINANCIAL REPORTING In many respects as important as financial reporting, this information would include such facts as how many clients were served, program participation, and numbers of programs. Reports on data required by national affiliates and funders also may be needed. Types and styles of reports will vary from organization to organization.

Much non-financial information is not easily reduced to numerical summation and reporting systems may need to be created. Records of program activities-such as numbers of members and non-members helped- are a primary area of interest. Calendars of organization events are particularly pertinent. Maintenance and repair schedules, inventories, and professional licensing requirements are other types of useful information for the board. Non-financial audits should be conducted, such as periodic independent review of employee files to be sure all necessary forms and reports are present and properly completed.

RESOURCE UTILIZATION Analyzing activities to make sure that the resources available to the organization are being fully and properly utilized starts with the budget. Monitoring the use of funds versus the budgeted use is a must and is more complicated than might first appear. Such monitoring also includes examination of how facilities are used-or, often, underused. Use of people in an organization, particularly where there are a number of volunteers, is an ongoing challenge to measure. Relatively established methods exist to review the performance of paid staff. All non-profits strive to fully utilize volunteers.

The area of collaborator utilization is relatively new. It should be, in many respects, relatively easy to measure. The chief indicators are how many collaborators are helping the organization, how the collaborated activities are performing, and how the individual collaborator's participation is changing- are more funds, people, and facilities by the collaborator being provided over time?

PROGRAM REVIEW The programs of any non-profit organization need to be reviewed constantly- for content, participation, and purpose. Relevance not only to the times, but more importantly to the goals of the organization, should be a continuing concern for the board. Growth, proportionate use of organization resources, and leadership availability are but some of the criteria to consider. Regular responsibility for this analysis and reporting needs to be clear.

OBSERVATIONS

- The documents in this following section are examples of reports that npos should evaluate for required and valuable use.

- A proprietary survey of board members representing over 100 npos indicates that a substantial majority of these board members have never had training from the organizations they represent in how to read financial statements.

- The challenge of quantifying relationships – the backbone of npo activities – for reporting purposes can be initially addressed by measuring the number of people and amount of time involved in any single activity. Qualifications of the people and the particular segments of time can be used for refinement of quantification and eventual calculation of financial implications.

- Understanding the "non-financial journal" of the organization – an integrated calendar/planner; here called a "log"– is an important step to understanding the availability and potential allocation of organization resources. The author believes that the periodic reporting of the non-financial journal of the organization to the board is second in importance only to the financial statements for giving the board an understanding of the organization's resource allocation and activities. Very few smaller npos currently report a non-financial journal regularly to the board.

- Frequently an npo does not have an Internal Audit Committee. Such a committee can save money and cover areas – such as audit of personnel files – that may not be covered otherwise.

- Minutes of Board meetings are the prime legal record of Board activities. The Board must be certain that minutes are complete and accurate.

- Many states require npos to register as fund-raising organizations as well as obtaining licenses to do business in the state. Separate processes and fees are involved in these two different filings.

- With increasing awareness and concern on the federal level for actions of organization boards, expect increasing regulation on the state level as well. Non-profits are not the primary focus at this time, but they will be addressed more and more as time goes on. Certain federal requirements – such as having a specific whistle blower policy and a formal document destruction policy – are already applicable to npos as well. Npos must be pro-active in keeping up to date on the regulatory front as communication on these matters is often slow and inefficient at the state level.

◆ NON-FINANCIAL JOURNAL (LOG)

ACTIVITY SCHEDULED	ORIGIN DATE	FINISH DATE	ACTUAL FINISH
Boardsmanship Seminar			
Audit			
Senior Trip to Museum			
Well Mother Retreat			
Staff meeting			
Licensing exam/h.c. profs			
Client picnic			
City inspection			
Property insurance renew			
National report due			
1090 filing due			
Repaint offices			
Bus annual inspection			
Driver training			
Health inspection			
Fed personnel audit			
State Licensing Board			
Memorial Day Holiday			
Volunteer Apprec. Dinner			
Annual Fund Drive			
Walk for Wellness			
Grants Conference			
Board meeting			
Annual Senior Staff Retreat			
Inventory supplies			
Publicity campaign			
Concert of Caring			
Breakfast for Tots			
Personnel reviews			
United Way campaign			
Founder's Day			
Annual Client Play			
Association Convention			
Strategic Planning Session			
Major Donor meeting			

DOCUMENTS TO BE FILED					
DOCUMENT	FREQ *	FED	STATE	LOCAL	SELF
ART. OF INCORP	1 + AM		X		
BY-LAWS	1 + AM				X
TAX-EXEMPTION	1 +	X			
BUS. LICENSE	A		X		
WORKMENS COMP	Q or A		X		
UNCEMP COMP	Q		X		
FED UNEMP COMP	Q or A	X			
SS (941, 944)	M or Q	X			
MED (941, 944)	M or Q	X			
FED WITHHOLD	M or Q	X			
990	A	X			
FED INCOME TAX	A	X			
STATE WITHHOLD	Q		X		
STATE INC TAX	A		X		
W-2s	A	X	X		
1099s	A	X	X		
NPO REGISTER	1 + AM		X		
CHARITY REGIS.	1 + AM		X		
PROF LICENSE	A?		?		
NATIONAL ORG	A?				
R. PROP TAXES	A			X	
P. PROP TAXES	A			X	
B & O TAXES	A?			X	
FIRE SERVICE	A			X	
VEHICLE LICENSE	A		X		
DOCUMENTS TO BE MAINTAINED					
PERSONNEL FILES	1 + AM				X
W BLOWER POL	1 + AM				X
DOC DE'RUCT POL	1 + AM				X

BD MTG MINUTES	M OR Q				X
RECOMMENDED DOCUMENTS					
AUDIT	A?				X
PERSONNEL MAN	1 + AM				X
'EE CONTRACTS	1 + AM				X
INSURANCE	A				X
DONOR RECEIPTS	A				X
JOB DESCRIPT'S	1 + AM				X
BD MEMBER J DES	1 + AM				X
COM'TEE J DECRIP	1 + AM				X
BOARD MANUAL	1 + AM				X
COPIES SHOULD BE KEPT OF ALL OUTSIDE FILINGS					
*AM=AMENDMENT, Q=QUARTERLY, M=MONTHLY, A=ANNUALLY					

These are, in most cases, categories of documents that will vary from year to year or amendment to amendment as the case may be. Also, in most cases, there are expected to be major variations not only in the content, but also in the form, of the individual documents from organization to organization. In other words, there is more than one "right" way to structure most of these documents; that they exist is often as important as what they contain. Frequency of filing may depend on the amount of dollars involved with certain federal and state filings.

Also, this is not a complete list in that required documents may vary from jurisdiction to jurisdiction and organization to organization (e.g., sales tax filings are made by some nonprofits) and some documentation that should be kept as a matter of good management practice may not exist for all organizations or may not be a priority for small organizations. These documents would include the following:

Contracts
Legal actions
Policies and procedures
Grievances
Paid invoices
Warranties and guarantees
Service contracts
Property titles
Strategic plans
Grant funding documentation
Licenses
Safety notices
Publicity
Indemnification agreements

Parental permission slips/powers of attorney
Bank account signature cards
Doctors' notices of illness/disability

In addition, there are documents that may be needed as good management practice which could have legal implications; you may not need them unless you don't have them. These would include such things as evidence of citizenship for employees, reference checks for employees and volunteers, and evidence of good business standing for suppliers and vendors to the organization.

Another important consideration is the length of time that various records should be kept; again, in some cases a matter of law and in others just good governance practices. An excellent starting point for length of time individual documents should be kept may be found in the "Non Profit Financials" review found in this book's addenda, that review's appendix b.

BEHAVIOR

LEGAL

SAFE

CONFIDENTIAL

ACCOUNTABLE

FAIR

COURTEOUS

BEHAVIOR

Behavior of an organization is the responsibility of the board. This responsibility means that the board must assure that standards are in place, processes exist to apply those standards, people are trained to properly carry out those processes, necessary resources are allocated, and that proper records are kept. Like other management duties, oversight of behavior on a daily basis usually resides with the CEO. Where the CEO duties may be divided and shared in certain respects, the board must be careful that monitoring behavior on a daily basis is appropriately assigned. The individual members of the board, of course, are the initial practitioners of behavior in an organization and must lead by example in this respect as in others. This discussion focuses on a division of organizational behavior into six categories.

LEGAL The board is responsible to make sure that the organization operates in a legal manner. Filings of necessary tax, employment, and other licenses, etc. are part of the legal oversight. Keeping required records properly, reporting requirements for special funding for programs or loans, retaining necessary documents on any grievances or lawsuits, and accounts of contributions are but some of the more common legal obligations. Proper recording of board minutes and committee meeting minutes may fall into this area as well. "Legal" in the organization may also cover requirements of any parent organization or affiliate for record keeping, notice filing, etc. Having the availability of legal counsel to the organization is a necessary resource.

SAFE Akin to legal operations, but going beyond is safe operations. The board must be aware of not only the legal requirements to behave safely, but also the common sense and beyond requirements. Regular training, notices, information and an emphasis as a priority for the organization are key components of safe operation. Risk management is a key responsibility for the CEO and the board must assure the availability of proper resources, including appropriate insurance programs.

CONFIDENTIAL In addition to the legal requirements for confidentiality for employee records, etc., there is a further obligation on the part of any organization to keep activities and decisions confidential. A common area for concern, and potential problems, is in the area of donations. Many donors do not want their contributions publicized and release of that information, even in an informal manner, may jeopardize future support from that donor as well as potential support from others. Personal opinions about others in the organization, if shared, may lead to conflict and a practice of "gossiping" that can destroy the ability of an organization to function. Obviously support for those in need should be confidential. Discretion is a must.

ACCOUNTABLE Too often those in leadership do not feel they need to fully report their activities to the stakeholders. In non-profits, where the staff and volunteers often come to think of themselves as a family, the trust and communication necessary to keep that family together requires full disclosure of decisions and activities where legal and confidential requirements permit. In addition, however, there are community and other interests that have a "right to know" to varying degrees on various matters. Such reporting may take the form of publicity that has other benefits. For some reporting, there may not be an established procedure with specific requirements – such as newsletter content and distribution. The board must keep in mind this responsibility and not be reluctant to share its thoughts and actions, along with the organization's.

FAIR In its actions, any organization must be fair – to staff, clients, members, etc. The culture of the organization must be applied to all, but exceptions to that culture should not give rise to discrimination. Different treatment of different employees and members should not take place. Usually this difference shows up in apparently little things which can assume major proportions and cause disruption. Invitation to outings, inclusion in distribution of organization perks, and use of organization facilities must be handled in a fair manner; usually this means that the process itself must be common knowledge and disclosed to all. An organization which behaves responsibly otherwise may not behave fairly and ultimately destroy itself as a result. This is a challenge for the board to meet for which there are not always concrete guidelines.

COURTEOUS Any organization should behave with courtesy. Courteous behavior begins with the board. The board of the organization must practice courtesy if the organization is to practice courtesy. The board members have an obligation to lead by example and to let the expectation of courteous behavior on the part of the CEO, staff, members and others be known.

OBSERVATIONS

- As in other areas of organization operation, expected behavior is best achieved by communication, training, and accountability through regular review. Few small organizations have regular training on expected behavior in dealing with clients and other stakeholders, particularly involving board members.

- A key area of behavior for board members revolves around organization meetings. Some "Tact Tips" are presented in this section. Common sense, which is the foundation for good behavior in meetings as well as other environments, is unfortunately not as common as might be hoped.

- A practical reason for focusing on issues and not personalities is that today's opposition in governance opinions is often tomorrow's ally – or potential ally.

- This section also includes excerpts on standards of conduct as well as conflicts of interest for Directors taken directly from the State of West Virginia's Non Profit Corporation Act. Easy research on the internet through any state's Secretary of State's office should lead readily to extant equivalent definitions.

- In addition to regularly scheduling planning sessions, a Board should periodically review articles of incorporation and by-laws. The author has seen established smaller organizations that are operating under authority that was never granted, as a corporation where none legally exists, and in a variety of other unintended circumstances that accomplish the organizaton's mission effectively and cause no problems until the organization is in crisis, at which point those circumstances quickly can become death knells at worst and budget breakers at best.

MEETING TACT TIPS

ARRIVE ON TIME, STAY UNTIL THE END

READ THE MATERIAL BEFORE YOU COME

TALK ABOUT ISSUES, NOT PEOPLE

DON'T SPEAK WHEN OTHERS ARE

GIVE OTHERS A CHANCE TO SPEAK

THERE ARE NO STUPID QUESTIONS

DON'T CRITICIZE THOSE NOT PRESENT

DISCLOSE CONFLICTS OF INTEREST

KEEP BUSINESS IN THE MEETING ROOM

NO SURPRISES

KEEP ON TOPIC

KEEP CONFIDENTIAL INFORMATION CONFIDENTIAL

HONOR COMMITTEE WORK

TAKE STAKEHOLDER CONCERNS TO CEO OUTSIDE MEETING,
LET CEO RESPOND

IT'S NOT ABOUT YOU!

WVC 31 E – 8 - 830

PART 3. DIRECTORS.

§31E-8-830. Standards of conduct for directors.

(a) Each member of the board of directors, when discharging the duties of a director, shall act: (1) In good faith; and (2) in a manner the director reasonably believes to be in the best interests of the corporation.

(b) The members of the board of directors or a committee of the board, when becoming informed in connection with their decision-making function or devoting attention to their oversight function, shall discharge their duties with the care that a person in a like position would reasonably believe appropriate under similar circumstances.

(c) In discharging board or committee duties a director, who does not have knowledge that makes reliance unwarranted, is entitled to rely on the performance by any of the persons specified in subdivisions (1) or (3), subsection (e) of this section to whom the board may have delegated, formally or informally by course of conduct, the authority or duty to perform one or more of the board's functions that are delegable under applicable law.

(d) In discharging board or committee duties a director, who does not have knowledge that makes reliance unwarranted, is entitled to rely on information, opinions, reports or statements, including financial statements and other financial data, prepared or presented by any of the persons specified in subsection (e) of this section.

(e) A director is entitled to rely, in accordance with subsection (c) or (d) of this section, on:

(1) One or more officers or employees of the corporation whom the director reasonably believes to be reliable and competent in the functions performed or the information, opinions, reports or statements provided;

(2) Legal counsel, public accountants, or other persons retained by the corporation as to matters involving skills or expertise the director reasonably believes are matters: (A) Within the particular person's professional or expert competence; or (B) as to which the particular person merits confidence; or

(3) A committee of the board of directors of which the director is not a member if the director reasonably believes the committee merits confidence.

WVC 31 E – 8 – 860

PART 6. DIRECTORS' CONFLICTING INTEREST TRANSACTIONS.

§31E-8-860. Directors' conflicting interest transactions.

(a) No contract or transaction between a corporation and one or more of its directors or officers, or between a corporation and any other corporation, partnership, association, or other organization in which one or more of its directors or officers are directors or officers, or have a financial interest, is void or voidable solely for this reason, or solely because the director or officer is present at or participates in the meeting of the board or committee thereof which authorizes the contract or transaction, or solely because any director's or officer's votes are counted for the purpose, if:

(1) The material facts as to the director's or officer's relationship or interest and as to the contract or transaction are disclosed or are known to the board of directors or the committee, and the board or committee in good faith authorizes the contract or transaction by the affirmative votes of a majority of the disinterested directors, even though the disinterested directors be less than a quorum; or

(2) The material facts as to the director's or officer's relationship or interest and as to the contract or transaction are disclosed or are known to the members entitled to vote on the contract or transaction, and the contract or transaction is specifically approved in good faith by vote of the members entitled to vote; or

(3) The contract or transaction is fair as to the corporation as of the time it is authorized, approved or ratified, by the board of directors, a committee of the board of directors, or the members.

(b) Common or interested directors may be counted in determining the presence of a quorum at a meeting of the board of directors or of a committee which authorizes the contract or transaction.

SELF-GOVERNANCE

RECRUITMENT AND TRAINING

ORGANIZATION MANAGEMENT

VOLUNTEER RECOGNITION

EVOLUTION

SELF-GOVERNANCE

The board is responsible for itself. Finding the best members and providing training, structuring the board as well as the organization, tracking and rewarding the contributions of members, and making needed changes in the composition, size, and organization of the board over time are up to the body itself. In some cases, guidelines and structure may be set out by a national parent. Implementing and supplementing them is the board's obligation. Four key areas are discussed here.

RECRUITMENT & TRAINING The process of nomination to the board and guidelines for candidate requirements and balance will vary from organization to organization. Size of the Nominating Committee, the procedure to be followed by the Committee in contacting candidates, and the particular added skills and experiences of candidates appropriate for the board at any given time are usually up to the board. Making sure that members go through any appropriate training desired is up to the board.

Evaluation of board member performance is a challenge for all non-profits; but evaluation of present board member performance is an important part of determining needs for added board members. For-profit organizations usually put that responsibility in the Nominating Committee. They use tools, such as board member job descriptions, attendance records, committee involvement, voting records and decorum as well as continued value of skills and experiences as measuring devices. Networking capabilities, including collaborative contacts, are important. Non-profits are moving into the same types of processes and mechanisms.

ORGANIZATION MANAGEMENT This discussion focuses on the board organization as a management responsibility of the board. Management of the whole organization as an organization will ultimately fall on the board as well, but the specifics of that management will depend on the size and goals of the organization. Detailed responsibility for the appropriate areas of management of the organization between the board and those allocated to the CEO need to be carefully thought out and spelled out in job descriptions and minutes.

Committee structure of the board usually is determined by the board. Size of the organization and board, activities, goals, and resources available are important determining factors in the board's decisions. The interaction between the board and committees is up to the board. Allocation of responsibilities to committees, either on a permanent or ad hoc basis, can determine if board meetings are long or short, primarily decision making or planning, devoted substantially to fellowship or primarily "business", or even harmonious or contentious. Conduct of meetings is board determined. Agendas need to be clear and distributed in advance. Times and places clearly must be set with sufficient notice and time limits set as well. Operating rules need to be clear and followed. Mutual respect must be exercised. Most organizations have adopted a version of Robert's Rules as their governing procedures. Familiarity with their content is necessary.

Certain tools for board governance can be extremely helpful. Ready availability of information about past board actions is important. This can be provided by creating "cross-references", such as a policy manual, that detail these past decisions without the need to search through sometimes years of board minutes if a question is raised; such as on a board's conflicts of interest policy. Individual member "job descriptions", committee chair job descriptions, staff job descriptions, committee membership directories and program descriptions are among the references which, if readily available, can make board meetings smoother.

VOLUNTEER RECOGNITION In non-profit management, this is a constant challenge. Although this discussion focuses on the board members as volunteers, almost all non-profits have the bulk of their volunteers as service volunteers, those who make the programs run on a daily basis. Recognizing and rewarding service volunteers is usually housed in the CEO position. Many varied methods are used. None of them could be considered the ultimate example.

Recognizing board volunteers is a separate challenge and almost non-existent in many non-profits. Placques on a wall listing names and years of service of past members are about as far as such recognition may go. Current practices fall short of what could be done and, arguably, should be done. Good examples are needed.

EVOLUTION All organizations go through changes and stages of existence. Non-profits are no exception. There has been some work done on the cycle of stages of some specialized organizations, such as churches. It is up to the board to research where the organization is, analyze changes desired, and lead the effort to make these changes. Differences in board size, committee structure, and staffing of the organization required by organization size and stage changes need to be an integral part of board planning and concern.

OBSERVATIONS

- Examples of records creation policy and standards of liability for Directors are reproduced here from the State of West Virginia Nonprofit Corporation Act. Easy research on the internet should determine any relevant state's equivalent requirements.

- Most smaller npos overlook the importance of keeping proper minutes. Remember that minutes are the legal record of what takes place at board meetings and the actions that derive from those decisions.

- Robert's Rules are the standard of guidance for board meeting conduct across our society. Keep in mind that they were not built with our typical npo in mind. Most of our npos' boards operate more by consensus than by strict Robert's Rules. In practice, when a board member starts to call upon Robert's Rules, disagreement and a potential fight are usually brewing. Most small npo board members have at best a superficial knowledge of Robert's Rules. We need meeting rules to operate and Robert's Rules are the most widely accepted standard we have, but the most effective nonprofits operate with an experienced Board Chair as the best way to keep meetings well run. It is worth checking to see if the governing State has any requirements in this area. West Virginia requires that the rules governing meetings be set out either in the Articles of Incorporation or the By-Laws; otherwise the Chair may set the meeting rules.

- The Nominating Committee procedures set out in this section are designed as a suggested process for internal operation of the Committee in selecting nominees. Other significant functions of the Nominating Committee – such as evaluating sitting board members, reviewing the overall board's profile of skills and experience in light of the Strategic Plan, and formalizing processes of identifying potential board members – will vary widely from organization to organization and go to the qualification of candidates for any particular openings. A well thought out set of procedures for an individual organization that covered all of these topics plus others pertinent to the organization – such as whether there should be a formal plan of succession among board officers – should be developed by each npo.

- Often candidates for a Nominating Committee position are not made aware in advance that the Nominating Committee is usually where responsibility rests for evaluating sitting board members as well as choosing new ones. Emphasis on corporate governance means that such evaluation is of increasing focus. Most non-profits do not practice even self-evaluation of board members, much less peer review, which is becoming a more wide-spread standard in the for-profit world and can be expected to apply to npos as well. Education as to expectations and follow-through are essential for the Board – and Nominating Committee – to adopt best practices in this area.

- New Board members should go through a formal orientation process. This process varies from organization to organization, with the CEO a key figure for smaller organizations. A sample list of the kinds of topics that should be detailed in an orientation process is set out in the following section.

NOMINATING COMMITTEE PROCEDURES

A. MEETINGS SHALL BE CALLED BY THE CHAIR AS NEEDED.

B. EACH VACANCY SHALL BE CONSIDERED SEPARATELY.

C. THE CHAIR SHALL CREATE A LIST OF ALL THOSE QUALIFIED TO FILL THE VACANCY WITH THE INPUT OF ALL MEMBERS OF THE COMMITTEE.

D. BY MAJORITY VOTE IF NECESSARY, THE COMMITTEE SHALL PRIORITIZE THE QUALIFIED PERSONS ACCORDING TO CRITERIA PREVIOUSLY ESTABLISHED BY THE GOVERNING BODY AND THE COMMITTEE.

E. THE CHAIR-OR SUCH INDIVIDUAL AS THE CHAIR SHALL DESIGNATE- SHALL THEN CONTACT THE QUALIFIED PERSONS IN THE ORDER IN WHICH THE COMMITTEE HAS PRIORITIZED THEM TO DETERMINE THEIR WILLINGNESS TO BE ELECTED. NO MORE PEOPLE SHALL BE CONTACTED THAN THERE ARE VACANCIES UNLESS A CLEAR ANSWER OF "NO" HAS BEEN OBTAINED, AT WHICH POINT THE NEXT PERSON ON THE PRIORITY LIST MAY BE CONTACTED.

F. NO MORE THAN ONE INDIVIDUAL MAY BE AUTHORIZED TO CONTACT CANDIDATES.

G. THE CHAIR WILL INFORM THE OTHER COMMITTEE MEMBERS AS SOON AS CANDIDATES HAVE AGREED TO ACCEPT NOMINATION TO ALL VACANCIES. THE COMMITTEE SHALL FORMALLY NOMINATE THESE CANDIDATES TO THE DECIDING BODY.

H. ALL DELIBERATIONS AND DISCUSSIONS OF THE COMMITTEE WILL BE HELD IN CLOSED MEETINGS WITH ALL PROCEEDINGS CONFIDENTIAL.

BOARD MEMBER JOB DESCRIPTION

❖ UNDERSTAND RESPONSIBILITIES OF A BOARD MEMBER

❖ UNDERSTAND ORGANIZATION'S MISSION, PROGRAMS AND POLICIES

❖ ATTEND BOARD MEETINGS PREPARED

❖ SERVE ON A STANDING COMMITTEE

❖ MAKE AN ANNUAL PERSONAL FINANCIAL CONTRIBUTION TO THE ORGANIZATION

❖ ATTEND SOCIAL FUNCTIONS SUPPORTING THE ORGANIZATION

❖ BE A PUBLIC SUPPORTER OF THE ORGANIZATION

❖ PARTICIPATE IN AT LEAST ONE ORGANIZATION SERVICE

COMMON CRITERIA FOR BOARD SERVICE

- ❖ PRESENT OR PAST BOARD SERVICE
- ❖ SERVICE TO THE ORGANIZATION
- ❖ SKILL SET
- ❖ COMMITMENT TO ORGANIZATION MISSION
- ❖ FINANCIAL SUPPORT OF THE ORGANIZATION
- ❖ STAKEHOLDER REPRESENTATION
- ❖ PARTICIPATION IN ORGANIZATION ACTIVITIES
- ❖ ADHERENCE TO PAST COMMITMENTS TO THE ORGANIZATION
- ❖ BOARD BALANCE
- ❖ COMPATIBILITY WITH PRESENT BOARD MEMBERS
- ❖ COMPATIBILITY WITH THE CEO AND STAFF
- ❖ WILLINGNESS TO BE AN ACTIVE MEMBER
- ❖ NETWORKING POTENTIAL
- ❖ PERSONAL CHARACTER
- ❖ SPECIALIZED KNOWLEDGE

BOARD COMMITTEE CHAIR JOB DESCRIPTION

❖ THE CHAIR SHALL BE A BOARD MEMBER AND MEET THE BOARD MEMBER JOB DESCRIPTION QUALIFICATIONS

❖ THE CHAIR MAY BE APPOINTED BY THE BOARD CHAIR OR ELECTED BY THE BOARD

❖ THE CHAIR MAY APPOINT NON BOARD MEMBERS TO THE COMMITTEE

❖ THE CHAIR CALLS COMMITTEE MEETINGS AND MODERATES COMMITTEE MEETINGS IN ACCORDANCE WITH THE MEETING RULES OF THE ORGANIZATION

❖ THE CHAIR REPORTS COMMITTEE WORK AND RECOMMEN-DATIONS TO THE BOARD

❖ THE CHAIR ASSIGNS COMMITTEE WORK TO COMMITTEE MEMBERS AND COORDINATES THE COMPLETION OF THAT WORK

❖ THE CHAIR IS THE COMMITTEE PERSON AUTHORIZED TO SIGN ON BEHALF OF THE COMMITTEE WHERE WRITTEN COMMITTEE OR CHAIR APPROVAL IS REQUIRED

❖ THE CHAIR IS RESPONIBLE FOR SEEING THAT ANY BUDGET RESPONSIBILITY OF THE COMMITTEE IS CARRIED OUT IN AN EFFECTIVE AND EFFICIENT MANNER

COMMITTEE STRUCTURE AND RESPONSIBILITY MAY BE SET FORTH IN THE BYLAWS AND SUPPLEMENTED BY OPERATING RULES ADOPTED BY THE BOARD. IN THE ABSENCE OF SPECIFIC GOVERNING BYLAWS OR OPERATING RULES, THE CHAIRMAN OF THE BOARD IN A DULY CALLED MEETING HAS SOME RIGHTS TO CREATE AND SUPERVISE BOARD COMMITTEES.

WVC 31 E – 15 - 1501

PART 1. RECORDS.

§31E-15-1501. Corporate records.

(a) A corporation shall keep as permanent records minutes of all meetings of its members and board of directors, a record of all actions taken by the members or board of directors without a meeting, and a record of all actions taken by a committee of the board of directors in place of the board of directors on behalf of the corporation.

(b) A corporation shall maintain appropriate accounting records.

(c) A corporation or its agent shall maintain a record of its members, if any, in a form that permits preparation of a list of the names and addresses of all members, in alphabetical order.

(d) A corporation shall maintain its records in written form or in another form capable of conversion into written form within a reasonable time.

(e) A corporation shall keep a copy of the following records at its principal office:

(1) Its articles or restated articles of incorporation and all amendments to them currently in effect;

(2) Its bylaws or restated bylaws and all amendments to them currently in effect;

(3) Resolutions adopted by its board of directors;

(4) The minutes of all members' meetings, and records of all action taken by members without a meeting, for the past three years;

(5) All written communications to members generally within the past three years, including the financial statements furnished for the past three years under section one thousand five hundred twenty of this article; and

(6) A list of the names and business addresses of its current directors and officers.

WVC 31 E – 8- 831

§31E-8-831. Standards of liability for directors.

a) A director is not liable to the corporation or its members for any decision to take or not to take action, or any failure to take any action, as a director, unless the party asserting liability in a proceeding establishes that:

(1) Any provision in the articles of incorporation authorized by subdivision (4), subsection (b), section two hundred two, article two of this chapter or the protections afforded by section eight hundred sixty of this article or article seven-c, chapter fifty-five of this code, if interposed as a bar to the proceeding by the director, does not preclude liability; and

(2) The challenged conduct consisted or was the result of:

(A) Action not in good faith; or

(B) A decision: (i) Which the director did not reasonably believe to be in the best interests of the corporation; or (ii) as to which the director was not informed to an extent the director reasonably believed appropriate in the circumstances; or

(C) A lack of objectivity due to the director's familial, financial or business relationship with, or a lack of independence due to the director's domination or control by, another person having a material interest in the challenged conduct: (i) Which relationship or which domination or control could reasonably be expected to have affected the director's judgment respecting the challenged conduct in a manner adverse to the corporation; and (ii) after a reasonable expectation has been established, the director does not establish that the challenged conduct was reasonably believed by the director to be in the best interests of the corporation; or

(D) A sustained failure of the director to devote attention to ongoing oversight of the affairs of the corporation, or a failure to devote timely attention, by making or causing to be made appropriate inquiry, when particular facts and circumstances of significant concern materialize that would alert a reasonably attentive director to the need to make inquiry; or

(E) Receipt of a financial benefit to which the director was not entitled or any other breach of the director's duties to deal fairly with the corporation and its members that is actionable under applicable law.

(b) The party seeking to hold the director liable:

(1) For money damages, has the burden of establishing that:

(A) Harm to the corporation or its members has been suffered; and

(B) The harm suffered was proximately caused by the director's challenged conduct; or

(2) For other money payment under a legal remedy, including compensation for the unauthorized use of corporate assets, has whatever persuasion burden may be called for to establish that the payment sought is appropriate in the circumstances; or

(3) For other money payment under an equitable remedy, including profit recovery by or disgorgement to the corporation, has whatever persuasion burden may be called for to establish that the equitable remedy sought is appropriate in the circumstances.

(c) Nothing contained in this section may: (1) In any instance where fairness is at issue, including consideration of the fairness of a transaction to the corporation under section eight hundred sixty of this article, alter the burden of proving the fact or lack of fairness otherwise applicable; (2) alter the fact or lack of liability of a director under another section of this chapter, including the provisions governing the consequences of an unlawful distribution under section eight hundred thirty-three of this article or a transactional interest under section eight hundred sixty of this article; or (3) affect any rights to which the corporation or a member may be entitled under another provision of this code or the United States code.

ORIENTATION

BOARD MEMBER DIRECTORY
BOARD MEMBER JOB DESCRIPTION
BOARD OFFICERS JOB DESCRIPTIONS
STAFF DIRECTORY
TABLE OF ORGANIZATION
MOST RECENT FINANCIALS
PROGRAMS SUMMARY
MISSION STATEMENT
VISION STATEMENT
TIME, PLACE, DURATION OF MEETINGS
STRATEGIC PLAN
KEY POLICIES
ORGANIZATION CALENDAR
COPY OF LIABILITY COVERAGE

AFTERWORD

This introduction to the responsibilities of board members is the first step on a governance path trod by constantly evolving companion egos in an atmosphere of ideas and enthusiasm. Next steps include education in particular knowledge areas necessary to carry out responsibilities – knowledge of such areas as understanding financial statements, how to raise funds, best practices in how to deliver the particular services provided by any one npo or fpo, and the legal intricacies of various applicable jurisdictions. A subtle barrier to board member education is the industry appellation of this process as "training", which is too often associated with rote learning. Perhaps the best approach is to treat this education as training in how to think in each of the subject areas. There is a world to be learned in ways to implement growing knowledge of best governance practices.

The second element in the governance mix is the interplay of egos that is constantly fluctuating in board meetings, service delivery, planning and any other activity that brings individuals together. We all learn how to deal with this mix in our daily lives – sometimes more successfully than others. Serving on a board with other volunteers brings its own aspects of this interplay of egos and often has the characteristics of a family discussion and decision process as opposed to a parliamentary one, yet the process is usually regulated by parliamentary rules. Behavior of boards and board members is a field of psychological analysis and study that is behind other areas such as crowd psychology and family psychology in the understanding of the average volunteer. The good news is that simply by becoming adults in our society, most of us have a learned understanding of how to act in most situations. There is much work that could be done, however, by the pertinent professionals to enlighten us and better guide us in how to deal with a wide variety of egos in the context of volunteer service and organization governance.

Perhaps the most exciting aspect of the governance mix is the development and use of ideas. Ideas bring the fire of enthusiasm for the mission and the energy to pursue the mission on the part of volunteers. At appropriate times (such as in the planning process) there are "no bad ideas" and it is to give opportunity for expression and reconciliation of ideas that is a prime motivator for frequency of planning sessions that include various stakeholders. In the for profit world, there has existed for a long time the formal practice of "brainstorming", which has yet to become widespread in the npo world. The volunteer board member has to learn to be not only a good manager, but also a good "imaginer".

ADDENDA

The first addendum is a discussion of nonprofit financials prepared by Louis J. Costanzo, III, CPA.

The second addendum is a synopsis of the West Virginia Nonprofit Corporation Act.

NON-PROFIT FINANCIAL INFORMATION

THIS INFORMATION HAS BEEN PREPARED BY LOUIS J. COSTANZO, III, CPA. MR. COSTANZO IS A PAST PRESIDENT OF THE WEST VIRGINIA SOCIETY OF CPAS.

Brief Overview of Nonprofit Financial Information

1. WHAT IS A NONPROFIT ORGANIZATION?

The accounting definition is as follows:

An entity that possesses the following characteristics that distinguish it from a business enterprise: (a) contributions of significant amounts of resources from resource providers who do not expect commensurate or proportionate pecuniary return, (b) operating purposes other than to provide goods or services at a profit, and (c) absence of ownership interests like those of business enterprises. Not-for-profit organizations have those characteristics in varying degrees. Organizations that clearly fall outside of this definition include all investor-owned enterprises and entities that provide dividends, lower costs or other economic benefits directly and proportionately to their owners, members or participants, such as mutual insurance companies, credit unions, farm and rural electric cooperatives and employee benefit plans.

Some examples of nonprofit organizations under the accounting definition are:

Cemetery organizations

Civic and community organizations

Colleges and universities

Elementary and secondary schools

Federated fund-raising organizations

Fraternal organizations

Labor unions

Libraries

Museums

Other cultural organizations

Performing arts organizations

Political parties

Political action committees

Private and community foundations

Professional associations

Public broadcasting stations

Religious organizations

Research and scientific organizations

Social and country clubs

Trade associations

Voluntary health and welfare organizations

Zoological and botanical societies

Salvation Army*

Red Cross*

Care*

Goodwill Industries*

United Way*

Boy Scouts and Girl Scouts*

*Also classified as a voluntary health and welfare organization.

THE INTERNAL REVENUE SERVICE (IRS) DEFINITION OF NONPROFITS IS AS FOLLOWS:

A nonprofit or tax-exempt organization is an organization exempt from income taxes, primarily under Section 501 of the Internal Revenue Code (IRC). Section 501 includes specified types of exempt organizations, such as charitable, religious and educational institutions; civic leagues; social clubs, etc. Most nonprofit organizations must apply for and receive recognition of tax-exempt status from the IRS. Churches, however, do not need to apply for tax-exempt status, but automatically qualify under IRC Section 501 (c) (3). Oftentimes, the only attribute shared by nonprofit organizations is their tax-exempt status; their missions and primary activities may be very diverse.

TYPES OF NONPROFIT ORGANIZATIONS

IRS Classification – There are more than 20 categories of tax-exempt organizations classified under Section 501 (c) of the Internal Revenue Code as well as additional types of organizations under other sections of the Code. Some of the major IRC Section 501 (c) classifications include the following:

- 501 (c) (3) – Organizations that are religious, educational, charitable, scientific or literary, or that test for public safety or foster national or international amateur sports competitions, or organizations for the prevention of cruelty to children or animals, the nature of whose activities is implied by the description of the class of organization.

- 501 (c) (4) – Civic leagues, social welfare organizations and local associations of employees, whose activities include promotion of community welfare along charitable, educational or recreational lines.

- 501 (c) (5) – Labor, agricultural and horticultural organizations, whose activities are educational or instructive, with the purpose of improving conditions of work or improving products and efficiency.

- 501 (c) (6) – Business leagues, chambers of commerce, real estate boards, etc., whose activities are intended to improve business conditions of one or more lines of business.

- 501 (c) (7) – Social and recreation clubs, the purpose of whose activities are pleasure, recreation and social.

Those are just some of the classifications of tax-exempt organizations under the IRC.

2. OBJECTIVES OF NONPROFIT ACCOUNTING AND FINANCIAL REPORTING:

The objectives of financial reporting for nonprofit organizations differ from those of business enterprises. The main objective of financial reporting for business enterprises is to provide information about an enterprise's performance as measured by earnings. The objectives of financial reporting for nonprofit organizations are to provide information to current and potential resource providers and others in assessing (a) the services a nonprofit organization provides and its ability to provide those services and (b) how management has discharged its stewardship responsibilities, as well as providing information about (c) the organization's economic resources, obligations and net resources and (d) the effects of transactions, events and circumstances that change those resources (i.e., the organization's performance or service efforts and accomplishments). More specifically, nonprofit financial reporting objectives are to –

   a. communicate the ways resources have been used to meet the organization's objectives and external requirements,
   b. identify an organization's principal programs and their costs,
   c. disclose the degree of control exercised by donors and funding sources over use of resources, and
   d. help the user evaluate the organization's ability to carry out its fiscal objectives.

More specifically, the purpose of nonprofit financial reporting is to provide information about –

   a. the amount and nature of an organization's assets, liabilities and net assets;
   b. transactions and other events and circumstances that affect net assets;
   c. the amount and kinds of inflows and outflows of economic resources during a period and the relationship between the inflows and outflows;
   d. an organization's cash revenues, support and expenses; its borrowing and repayment of borrowing; and other factors that may affect its liquidity; and
   e. the service efforts of an organization.

Groups that are particularly interested in the financial information of a nonprofit organization include the following:

   f. Funding sources and contributors in the organization.
   g. Regulatory agencies.
   h. Governing boards (board of trustees or directors).
   i. Beneficiaries of the services rendered by the organization.
   j. Employees.
   k. Creditors and potential creditors.
   l. Constitutional organizations, e.g., a local chapter or a national organization.

3   ACCRUAL BASIS ACCOUNTING OR CASH BASIS ACCOUNTING

Under the procedures of accrual basis accounting, the organization records those events that affect its financial statements in the periods in which those events occur, rather than only in those periods in which, as a result of those events, the organization receives or pays cash. For example, using the accrual basis to measure performance for the period means recognizing revenues when earned rather than when cash is received and recognizing expenses when incurred rather than when paid.

Capturing financial transactions and events in the periods in which they occur provides the organization the opportunity to accurately identify its financial position at the end of a reporting period and the results of its operations during the period. Accurate statements of revenues earned and expenses incurred support meaningful comparisons between actual operations and the budget established for the period. Cash-based accounting, which recognizes revenue only on receipt of cash and expenses only on disbursement of cash, ignores uncollected revenues and unpaid expenses and thus eliminates the possibility of meaningfully reporting against a budget.

Many smaller organizations maintain their books on a cash basis during the fiscal year and adjust affected balances to the accrual basis at fiscal year end. While financial statements prepared at year end will conform to the accrual basis, interim financial statements will lack the capacity to measure performance in meaningful ways and may fail to provide information necessary to the determination of desirable mid-course changes in planned operations. Finally, if large revenue and expense items are not treated on the accrual basis, comparisons with the operating budget for the period may be difficult to make.

One easily accomplished option is to treat certain revenue and expense items on the accrual basis and others on a cash basis. For example, small items of revenue and expense may be treated on the cash basis throughout the year without distorting the financial statements provided that large items are treated on the accrual basis. This "modified accrual basis" accounting has the advantage of simplicity without creating material distortion.

4.   FUND ACCOUNTING CAN STILL BE USED IN NONPROFIT ACCOUNTING:

PROCEDURES OF FUND ACCOUNTING

Fund accounting is the procedure by which resources received are classified into discrete funds (distinct accounting entities) according to the specific limitations imposed upon their use either by donors (limitations = restrictions) or by the governing body (limitations = designations). Further bases for classification include specific activities or objectives, the nature of the resources included or the manner in which a specific group of resources is managed by the organization.

Each fund comprises a self-balancing set of accounts including assets, liabilities, revenues, gains, expenditures, losses, transfers and fund balance. Asset and liability accounts reflect the specific resources committed to the fund and the obligations of the fund, respectively. Revenue, gain, expenditure, loss and transfer accounts capture the ongoing activities recorded in the fund. The fund balance is the difference between a fund's assets and liabilities. Changes in fund balance represent the difference between resources inflows (revenues, gains and transfers-in) and outflows (expenditures, losses and transfers-out).

As a consequence of the definitions of assets, liabilities and fund balance, it is an accounting identity that

Assets = liabilities + fund balance

Accordingly, fund balance = assets − liabilities. Fund balance may be regarded as the fund's residual interest in its assets after the interests of others (liabilities) have been deducted. These relationships apply at both the individual fund level and the aggregate of all funds, or the organizational level.

Typically, organizations classify institutional resources into at least three fund groups with subgroups in each as follows:

Current funds – include those resources available to support the primary purposes of
the organization.

Current Unrestricted Fund – includes resources received by the organization that have no stipulations or limitations placed on them by external donors. Typically, resources in this group include all earned revenues, unrestricted gifts received and unrestricted endowment and investment income.

Current Restricted Fund – includes resources provided to an organization by external donors who have restricted the use of their gifts to specific operating purposes. Resources accounted for in this fund also include endowment income that has been restricted by the donor of the endowment to specific operating purposes.

Plant funds – include those resources committed to acquiring, improving and
maintaining the physical plant of the organization. (Ordinary occupancy costs – rent, utilities, maintenance and repair, etc. – are recognized as expenditures of the Current Unrestricted Fund.) Gifts received from donors who have stipulated that their contributed resources benefit these functions are also recorded in the plant funds group.

Unexpected Plant Fund – includes all liquid resources available to acquire, improve, replace or renew the physical plant of the organization. Typically, gifts restricted to plant acquisition or improvement are included in this fund. The PPRRSM account (Provision for Plant Renewal, Replacement and Special Maintenance) funded by transfers-in from the Current Unrestricted Fund is also maintained in this fund as are other unrestricted reserves that may have been designated by the governing board for purposes of aquiring specific plant items.

Investment in Plant Fund - comprises the "inventory" of the organization's fixed assets including assets held under capital leases (land, buildings, equipment, leased autos and computers accounted for as capital leases, etc.), related depreciation and any debt thereon (including mortgages, notes payable secured by plant assets and capital lease liabilities). Gifted plant assets (gifts-in-kind) are also recognized in this fund.

Fund for Retirement of Indebtedness – comprises liquid resources accumulated for the purpose of retiring mortgages or other debt secured by plant assets. Both unrestricted assets transferred-in from the Current Unrestricted Fund and gifts restricted to this purpose may be accommodated within the fund. This fund is often subsumed within the Unexpected Plant Fund.

ENDOWMENT AND SIMILAR FUNDS

Endowment Fund – comprises gifts received with the donor-imposed stipulation that the principal of the gift be retained intact in perpetuity. The donor may further stipulate that the investment return (interest, dividends and net gains) on the gift principal be restricted to a particular operating purpose and/or that some portion of the return be reinvested as additional principal for the purpose of protecting the historical gift value from the eroding effects of inflation.

Term Endowment Fund – comprises gifts received with the donor-imposed stipulation that the principal of the gift be retained for a specific period of time or until the occurrence of a stipulated event after which the gift principal is reclassified to permanent endowment or some other use. Frequently, donors require reinvestment of return during the holding period of a term endowment gift.

Quasi-Endowment Fund (Funds Functioning as Endowment) – comprises unrestricted assets designated by the governing board for long-term investment with earnings designated to support unrestricted operations. Balances included in the Quasi-Endowment Fund are transferred from the Current Unrestricted Fund. Since the "corpus" of the Quasi-Endowment Fund is unrestricted, the balance of the fund is available for appropriation by simple determination of the governing board.

OTHER FUND GROUPS

Agency Funds – comprise moneys on deposit with the organization which are held on behalf of others; the organization has custody of the funds but not little to them.

Annuity, Pooled and Life Income Funds – comprise the corpus of and transactions associated with split-interest gifts.

INTERFUND TRANSACTIONS

As noted, the technique of fund accounting treats the organization as if it were a set of discrete operating segments, a series of managed asset groups. Since the operations of any organization are highly integrated, it is necessary that the different funds included within the general ledger be able to "do commerce" with each other. This is accomplished through the use of two specific account pairings, the nature of the transaction determining which of the pairings is used.

Due From/Due to Other Funds – an asset/liability account pairing. When the underlying transaction is one in which one fund receives or expends money on behalf of another fund and the expectation is of future resource repatriation, the transaction is viewed as an interfund loan.

5. FROM FUND ACCOUNTING TO CURRENT ACCOUNTING REQUIREMENTS:

Under SFAS 117, the emphasis shifts from how assets are managed within the organization to the organization as-a-whole and the availability or expendability of its net resources. Thus, all of the assets, liabilities and net assets of the organization must be aggregated for financial statement reporting purposes. Then, within net assets, the availability or expendability of net resources is disclosed by dividing the organization's net assets into three distinct classes.

1. Permanently restricted net assets

Permanently restricted net assets is the part of the net assets of a not-for-profit organization resulting (a) from contributions and other inflows of assets whose use by the organization is limited by donor-imposed stipulations that neither expire by the passage of time nor can be fulfilled or otherwise removed by actions of the organization, (b) from asset enhancements and diminishments subject to the same kinds of stipulations, and (c) from reclassifications from (or to) other classes of net assets as a consequence of donor-imposed stipulations.

2. Temporarily restricted net assets

Temporarily restricted net assets is the part of the net assets of a not-for-profit organization resulting (a) from contributions and other inflows of assets whose use by the organization is limited by donor-imposed stipulations that either expire by passage of time or can be fulfilled and removed by actions of the organization pursuant to those stipulations, (b) from other asset enhancements and diminishments subject to the same kinds of stipulations, and (c) from reclassifications to (or from) other classes of net assets as a consequence of donor-imposed stipulations, their expiration by passage of time, or their fulfillment and removal by actions of the organization pursuant to those stipulations.

3. Unrestricted net assets

Unrestricted net assets is the part of net assets of a not-for-profit organization that is neither permanently restricted nor temporarily restricted by donor-imposed stipulations – that is, the part of net assets resulting (a) from all revenues, expenses, gains and losses that are not changes in permanently or temporarily restricted net assets and (b) from reclassifications from (or to) other classes of net assets as a consequence of donor-imposed stipulations, their expiration by passage of time or their fulfillment and removal by actions of the organization pursuant to those stipulations. The only limits on unrestricted net assets are broad limits resulting from the nature of the organization.

A consequence of the emphasis in SFAS 117 on the organization as-a-whole and the expendability of its net resources is the replacement of fund accounting's "fund balance" with SFAS 117's "net assets". While both describe the residual interest of an entity in its assets after deducting its liabilities, the entity of fund accounting is the fund; the entity of SFAS 117 is the organization.

Within the emphasis in SFAS 117 on aggregation and the organization as-a-whole, individual assets and liabilities are not regarded as restricted or unrestricted; only the organization's net assets are so classified. Note that within the disaggregated approach of conventional fund accounting, assets and liabilities are assigned to and regarded as belonging to the separate funds. Thus, in fund accounting, restrictions and designations apply to specific assets.

For purposes of financial statement presentation, the discrete funds of the general ledger are consolidated into the net asset categories of SFAS 117. The table in Appendix A displays the groupings of funds that fit within each net asset class.

6. GENERAL PURPOSE FINANCIAL STATEMENTS:

The concept of "general purpose financial statements" is important because the general purpose financial statements represent what is generally accepted as the end product of a nonprofit organization's financial accounting process.

WHAT IS INCLUDED IN GENERAL PURPOSE FINANCIAL STATEMENTS?

Financial Accounting Standards require the general purpose financial statements for nonprofit organizations to include:

- A statement of financial position.
- A statement of activities
- A statement of functional expenses (required for voluntary health and welfare organizations only).
- A statement of cash flows.
- Notes to financial statements.

See samples of these financial statements in Appendix B.

COMPARATIVE FINANCIAL STATEMENTS

The accounting literature also recommends that comparative financial statements be presented.7.   **GAAP:**

Generally accepted accounting principles (GAAP) apply to all financial statements (except statements presented on an other comprehensive basis of accounting) and are relevant to all accountants (whether in nonprofit organizations or public accounting) who are concerned with producing meaningful financial statements.

WHAT IS GAAP?

While accountants agree on the existence of a body of knowledge called GAAP, the determination that a particular accounting principle is generally accepted may be difficult because no single reference source exists for all such principles.

GAAP in general terms is a technical accounting term that encompasses the conventions, rules and procedures necessary to define accepted accounting practice at a particular time. It includes not only broad guidelines of general application, but also detailed practices and procedures. Those conventions, rules and procedures provide a standard by which to measure financial presentations.

8. BUDGETING CONCEPTS AND PROCEDURES:

THE ANNUAL BUDGET

The annual operating budget of the organization reflects the intersection of programs and finances. It represents the most concrete reflection of organizational priorities.

There is no more important management tool in an organization than the budget for operating expenses and the related reporting of budgeted versus actual expenses. The budget is the financial embodiment of the annual planning process. Thus, the real purpose of the budgeting process is to decide upon the operating plan for the year. Regardless of the level of financial stringency in the organization, a thoughtful budget is essential to ensure that funds are used to achieve the highest possible level of effectiveness.

Stated most simply, a budget is an itemized estimate of inflows and outflows for a given period in the future. Obviously, such as estimate can cover a variety of periods and a variety of definitions of inflows and outflows. There are many kinds of budgets, such as the long-range planning budget, the capital budget and the cash budget. The capital budget normally covers the same one-year period as the operating budget but concerns purchases of long-lived assets.

INCREMENTAL VS. ZERO-BASED BUDGETING

Several considerations are involved in projecting next year's revenue and expense: the budget for this year, the estimated results for this year, the actual results for last year, the operating plans for next year and the forecast of two key variables – enrollment levels and inflation rates. A vital issue here is whether to use past data as a base for budgeting or to start entirely fresh each year.

A natural tendency is to take current spending levels as given and to concentrate only on proposed changes. This <u>incremental</u> approach usually results in devoting 85 to 90 percent of the time and effort to 15 to 10 percent of the dollars. A conceptually more appealing approach is to consider the justification for each dollar of expenditure each year. This process is called "<u>zero-based</u>" budgeting because it takes nothing as given. The base for a new budget is zero. Every dollar of expense must be defended anew each year. Zero-based budgeting is applied, at least in part, in both commercial and nonprofit organizations because it results in devoting the bulk of time and attention each year to the bulk of the dollars.

In practice, of course, it is not feasible to renounce all past commitments each year and start afresh. Past data are always of major importance to a new budget. As a concept, however, zero-based budgeting is sound. It should be kept firmly in mind each year lest past decisions be continually reaffirmed without full attention to their present applicability. One possible compromise is to schedule a detailed or zero-based review of some subset of budget items each year on a rotating basis. In this way, each item is reviewed carefully every few years. Even so, it should be kept in mind that past data may well be the most useful source of information on items that recur regularly from year to year.

For example, if the organization has borrowed money, it will have to pay a predetermined amount of interest on the loan. Short of finding some way to pay off the debt ahead of schedule, the organization has no choice about this expense. Almost as immutable are other items that have been programmed for a period of two or three years, such as an agreed-upon three-year schedule of premiums with a fire insurance company. Unless the situation changes markedly, this schedule fixes next year's expense.

9. CASH MANAGEMENT:

The primary tool in effective cash management is a comprehensive, up-to-date cash budget. A cash budget is different from an operating budget. The operating budget is a projection of the revenues the organization will earn and the expenses it will incur during the year. Progress in meeting the operating budget is monitored throughout the year as part of the cost control process, but it really is the difference between revenues and expenses for the year as whole that is important, not month-to-month differences.

THE CASH BUDGET

The cash budget is a twelve-month projection of all cash receipts and cash disbursements for the organization. It is important to keep in mind that cash receipts are not the same thing as revenues earned and that cash disbursements are not the same thing as expenses incurred. For example, some cash receipts this year do not represent earned revenue this year, as in the case of collection of prior years' tuition. Similarly, some of this year's revenue will not be collected in cash. Some cash disbursements do not represent operating expenses, as in the case of payments on mortgage principal. The cash budget is therefore very different, conceptually, from the operating budget, though both are important management tools.

Since the organization must maintain adequate cash balances at all times to pay bills as they fall due, cash receipts and disbursements must be monitored on a month-to-month basis. Thus, for the cash budget, month-to-month variations in cash inflows and outflows are equally as important as overall inflows and outflows for the year.

Preparing a monthly cash budget is quite simple. First, total anticipated cash receipts for the year are projected by month. Then, total anticipated cash disbursements for the year are projected by month. Projected month-to-month fluctuations in the cash balance are then calculated.

The next step is to consider how projected receipts might be accelerated or projected disbursements be postponed to avoid "red" balances in some months, to reduce the size of red balances wherever possible, or to increase the amount of excess cash, which can be invested temporarily. Red, or negative, cash balances in the projected cash budget indicate a need for short-term borrowing to finance the temporary deficit. While the timing of many receipt and disbursement items is not discretionary, other items do allow some flexibility in timing. Those items can be "managed" to produce a more advantageous overall cash flow picture.

Cash management program

An effective cash management program has three primary goals: (1) to get cash receipts as soon as possible, (2) to postpone cash disbursements as long as is prudent, and (3) to invest "excess" cash, while it is on hand, to earn a return.

10. INTERNAL CONTROLS:

A sound system of internal control is necessary to ensure that the organization carries out fully its stewardship responsibilities for the funds entrusted to it. Such a system also makes it easier to complete the annual audit in an orderly and timely fashion.

Effective internal accounting control is achieved through an integrated system of people, records and procedures. Creating a control environment is often a process of education. It must be clear from the attitude of trustees and administrators that effective controls are a matter of high priority. The organization's staff must then be made to understand the importance and philosophy of internal accounting control before an effective system can be created and maintained.

An adequate internal accounting control structure requires that the organization use specific methods and procedures to safeguard its assets, to check the accuracy and reliability of its accounting data, to promote operational efficiency, and to encourage adherence to prescribed policies. I suggest:

- A clear-cut plan that provides for definite placement of responsibility and for specific lines of authority.

- Division of duties, wherever practicable, between authorization and record keeping so that the activities of one employee act as a check on those of another.

- Forms, documents and procedures that provide for control and proper approvals.

- Monitoring for compliance with policies, procedures and budgets.

- Periodic formal review of the control system and its effective ness in relation to the ever-changing character of the organization and the environment.

CONTROL FROM THE TOP

The board of trustees and the management have ultimate responsibility for the internal accounting control structure. This responsibility is particularly important to organizations, where scarce resources often limit the extent of formal control systems. Management must have a clear understanding of responsibilities, monitor accounting records and procedures and review overall operations.

CONTROL OBJECTIVES

Internal accounting control objectives include control over authorization of transactions, recording of transactions, access to assets and asset accountability. Internal accounting controls should reflect the unique environment, attributes and risks inherent in the operation of the organization. Key control objectives for each major area of operation should be identified and set forth in writing.

SEGREGATION OF DUTIES

Segregation of duties is a fundamental component of a good internal accounting control structure. Nonprofit organizations often do not have sufficient personnel to achieve traditional segregation of duties. In such instances, active involvement of trustees and senior administrators is monitoring the course of activities and the flow of resources in and out of the organization is essential.

11. RECORDS RETENTION:

It is important for the organization to have a records management and retention program that will:

- Ensure protection of vital records in case of destruction by fire or some other catastrophic event.

- Assure compliance with state and federal laws governing retention of important records.

- Maintain confidentiality of financial and other restricted records.

- Release storage space by disposing of records no longer needed.

RECORDS MANAGEMENT CHECKLIST

The organization should look at how it currently handles and stores its records. Here are some questions to consider:

- Does the organization have a written policy on records management?

- Does the organization have a guide or schedule for retaining records that meets state and federal requirements and follows generally accepted procedures?

- Does the organization have a system for storing permanent records?

- Does the organization maintain a filing system that allows records to be filed and found easily?

- Does the organization have microfilm copies of essential paper records and backup disks or tapes of important computer records? Are these copies securely stored in a building separate from the originals – a bank vault or a record archive?

- Does the organization provide fireproof storage areas for permanent records?

- Does the organization have a systematic program for transferring or retiring inactive records?

TAKING A RECORDS INVENTORY

As a beginning point, it is strongly recommended that the organization take a physical inventory of all its records, which should provided the basis for an overall records program. The following information should be gathered.

- Location: number and name of department where the record is stored and of the department responsible for the record.

- Record title: invoices, address files, alumni(ae) files, etc.

- Type of record and quantity: file drawers, ledger books, folders, tapes, etc.

- Dates covered by a record (a particular set of records may be divided among several inventory cards on the basis of dates covered by the records).

- Need: essential? desirable? unneeded?

- Access: degree of confidentiality determines access to the record and method of storage.

- Second-copy decision: to be determined by the person taking the inventory; may also involve a recommendation on type of storage of second copy.

- Additional comments

- Signature and date

RETENTION SCHEDULE

Appendix C shows a suggested retention schedule for records. Individual state requirements and a particular organization's needs may dictate differing retention periods. The organization should consult its legal counsel when question arise.

12. DEALING WITH THE INDEPENDENT CERTIFIED PUBLIC ACCOUNTANT:

SERVICES PROVIDED BY THE CPA

Although the annual audit is the principal service provided by the independent auditor, he or she can also provide other services to the organization. Following is a summary of these services.

THE ANNUAL AUDIT

The primary service the CPA provides is the annual examination of the financial records. This examination should be conducted in accordance with the generally accepted auditing standards set by the Auditing Standards Board, which functions under the auspices of the American Institute of Certified Public Accountants. The annual audit involves an analytic review of the organization's operations, review and testing of the organization's internal control systems, tests for accuracy of the accounting records and verification of significant asset and liability balances. When the annual audit is completed, the auditor prepares a letter expressing an opinion about the financial statements of the organization

In addition to the auditor's opinion letter, the trustees may also receive each year, as a result of the audit, a commentary by the auditor on the overall financial management practices of the organization, with suggested improvements. Such commentary is typically called a "management letter".

Bookkeeping services

The CPA can take responsibility for maintaining the basic books of account for the organization, which includes recording all transactions and all necessary adjusting entries in the books of original entry and maintaining the general ledger.

Providing basic bookkeeping and accounting services is called "write up" work.

Periodic preparation or review of financial statements

If the financial record keeping is done by someone on the staff of the organization who is a bookkeeper but not an accountant, the CPA can take responsibility for preparing monthly or quarterly financial statements. Such interim information is of great value to the board of trustees in reviewing and monitoring results of operations as the year progresses. In constructing interim financial statements the CPA first reviews the books and records to make sure that all significant items are properly reflected.

Even if the organization's business officer is responsible for preparing the interim financial statements, the trustees sometimes deem it desirable to have the CPA review them periodically as an independent check on accuracy and significance. Such periodic review by the CPA also ensures that no accounting or reporting problems arise that might cause delay or other difficulties in the year end audit

Consulting and financial advisory services

The CPA can undertake specific consulting projects involving improvements to the basic accounting systems, the reporting system, financial controls, budgeting and financial planning systems, and systems for managing such items as cash, accounts receivable and accounts payable. The CPA's expertise as a financial professional and familiarity with the organization offer significant advantages when the organization is thinking about using a consultant.

APPENDIX A

The fund classifications of fund accounting readily articulate the net asset categories prescribed by SFAS 117.

Fund/Net Asset Class	Unrestricted Net Assets	Temporarily Restricted Net Assets	Permanently Restricted Net Assets
Current Unrestricted Fund	Economic resources available for any operating need. Includes earned revenues and gifts received without donor stipulation as to use.	N/A	N/A
Current Restricted Fund	N/A	Gifts received that are restricted by donors to specific operating purposes.	N/A
Unexpected Plant Fund	Includes unrestricted reserves designated by the board for plant purposes including reserves for renewal and replacement of plant and equipment assets (PPRRSM)	Includes gifts received that are restricted by donor stipulations to plant purposes (asset acquisition, retirement of debt, major renewal or renovation projects).	N/A
Investment in Plant Fund	Plant assets (land, buildings, equipment), Accumulated depreciation, related debt.	Certain plant assets may be classified as temporarily restricted if that option is elected.	Plant assets given under the stipulation that they be held for their useful lives and that proceeds on their ultimate disposition be invested in perpuity.
Endowment Fund	N/A	Term endowment funds require the principal of the gift to be invested for a specific period of time after which the funds are to be utilized in accordance with any further donor stipulations.	Gifts received under stipulation that the principal be retained intact in the perpetuity. Income on the investment of the principal may be restricted to specific operating purposes by the donor or remain unrestricted.

Quasi-Endowment Fund	Reserves accumulated for long-term investment purposes with income applied to general or designated operating purposes (Funds functioning as endowment).	N/A	N/A

APPENDIX B

RECORDS RETENTION GUIDELINES

Type of record	Retention period (yrs)	Type of record	Retention period (yrs)
Accounting		*Corporate (continued)*	
Auditor's reports	Permanent	Bylaws	Permanent
Audit work papers	5	Construction & major equipment records	Permanent
Bank deposit slips	3	Contract bids	3
Bank statements	3	Contract & trademark registration	Permanent
Budgets	2	Contracts & agreements	Permanent
Cancelled checks/ taxes	Permanent	Correspondence (gen.)	6
" " all other	8	" " (legal)	Permanent
Cash disbursement journals	Permanent	Deeds & easements	Permanent
Cash projections	2	Long-range plan study	9
Cash receipts journals	Permanent	Maintenance records	9
Contracts (purchases & sales)	3+	Minutes	Permanent
Credit memos	3	Mortgage agreements	6+
De[recitation records	3+	Fed. & State Reports	Permanent
Employee expense reports	6		
Endowment records & reports	**Permanent**	*Insurance*	
Financial statements annual	Permanent	Accident reports	6
Financial statements interim	3	Fire inspector reports	6
Freight bills	3	Group disability rec.	8
General journals	Permanent	Insurance policies	Permanent
General ledgers	Permanent	Safety records	8
Inventory lists	3	Settled insurance claim	10

Invoices	3		
Parent payments	**10**	*Personnel*	
Payroll records	8		
Petty cash vouchers	3	Employment records	5
Purchase journals	Permanent	Retirement/pension records	Permanent
Purchase orders	3	Personnel files	10 (after term.)
Purchase records	3	Sickness/disability rec.	6
Subsidiary ledgers Accounts Payable	6		
Subsidiary ledgers Accounts Receivable	**6**	*Student & alumni(ae)*	
Time cards & daily time reports	3	Academic performance records	6
Trial balances	6	Admission folders	2
		Comments/reports/ parents	**2**
Corporate		Fund-raising files	2
		Grade lists	2
IRS approval letters	Permanent	Transcripts	Permanent
Articles of Incorporation	Permanent	Yearbooks	Permanent
		Taxes	
		IRS approval letters	Permanent
		Payroll tax returns	6
		Sales & use tax returns	Permanent
		Withholding tax returns	6

These guidelines are taken from two sources: (1) a reprint from *Connecticut Business Times, June 1981,* and (2) information from the US Government Printing Office. In general, where variations occur, the more conservative number is used.

WV NONPROFIT CORPORATION ACT SYNOPSIS

31E-1-101, 102, 103: Short Title, Reservation of Powers, Construction of Chapter

31E-1-120, 121, 122: Filing requirements, Forms, Filing fees.

31E-1-123, 124: Effective time and date, Correcting filed document

31E-1-125, 126: Filing duty of secretary of state, Appeal from refusal to file

31E-1-127, 128: Evidentiary effect of copy of document, Certificate of existence

31E-1-129, 130: Penalty for signing false document, Powers of Secretary of State

31E-1-140, 150: Venue, Definitions

"Employee' includes an officer and may include a director: Provided, That the director has accepted duties that make him or her also an employee."
"Nonprofit corporation' means a corporation which may not make distributions to its members, directors or officers."

31E-1-151, 152: Notice, Number of members.

31E-2-201, 202, 203: Incorporators, Articles of Incorporation, Incorporation

"The articles of incorporation must set forth:
...(2) A statement that the corporation is nonprofit and that the corporation may not have or issue shares of stock or make distributions."

31E-2-204, 205, 206: Organization of corporation, Bylaws, Emergency Bylaws

"An emergency exists for purposes of this section if a quorum of the corporation's directors cannot readily be assembled because of some catastrophic event."

31E-3-301, 302, 303, 304: Purposes, General powers, Emergency powers, Ultra vires

"... for any lawful purpose..."
"... issue its notes, bonds, and other obligations..."
"To ...establish...profit sharing plans..."
"To carry on one or more businesses..."

31E-4-401, 402, 403, 404: Corporate name, Use of the words "corporation", "incorporated" or "limited", Reserved name, Registered name

'The provisions of this section do not apply to businesses in existence prior to the first day of July, one thousand nine hundred eighty-eight."

31E-5-501, 502, 503, 504: Registered office and agent, Change of registered office or agent, Resignation of registered agent, Service on corporation

31E-6-601, 602, 603, 604: Classes of members, Rules for membership, Imposition of fine and penalties: levy of dues and assessments, Liability of members

"A corporation may impose fines or penalties on members if provided in bylaws…"

31E-7-701, 702, 703: Annual meeting, regular meeting, Special meeting, Court-ordered meeting

"The failure to hold an annual or regular meeting at the time stated in or fixed in accordance with a corporation's bylaws does not affect the validity of any corporate action."

31E-7-704, 705, 706, 707: Action without meeting, Notice of meeting, Waiver of Notice, Record date

31E-7-708 Conduct of the meeting

"The chairperson, unless the articles of incorporation or bylaws provide otherwise, shall determine the order of business and has the authority to establish rules for the conduct of the meeting."

31E-7-720, 721, 722: Members' list for meeting, Members' voting rights, Proxies

31E-7-723, 724: Corporation's acceptance of votes, Quorum/voting requirements

"Once a member is represented for any purpose at a meeting, the member is deemed present for quorum purposes for the remainder of the meeting and for any adjournment of that meeting unless a new record date is or must be set for that adjourned meeting."

31E-7-725, 726: Action by single and multiple cases of members, Other quorum or voting requirement

31E-7-727, 728: Voting for directors; cumulative voting, Inspectors of election

31E-8-801: Requirement for and duties of board of directors

"All corporate powers are to be exercised by or under the authority of, and the activities, property and affairs of the corporation managed under the direction of, its board of directors, subject to any limitation set forth in the articles of incorporation."

31E-8-802, 803: Qualifications of directors, Number and election of directors

31E-8-804, 805: Special provisions regarding directors, Election of directors by certain classes of members

31E-8-806, 807: Terms of directors generally, Staggered terms for directors

31E-8-808, 809, 810: Resignation of directors, Removal of directors by members or directors, Removal of directors by judicial proceeding

31E-8-811, 812: Vacancy on board, Compensation of directors

"Unless the articles of incorporation or bylaws provide otherwise, the board of directors may fix the compensation of directors, including reasonable allowance for expenses actually incurred in connection with their duties."

31E-8-820, 821, 822, 823: Meetings, Action without meeting, Notice of meeting, Waiver of notice

31E-8-824, 825, 826: Quorum and voting, Committees, Court-ordered meeting of directors

"(d) A director who is present at a meeting of the board of directors or a committee of the board of directors when corporate action is taken is deemed to have assented to the action taken unless..."

"(f) The creation of, delegation of authority to, or action by a committee does not alone constitute compliance by a director with the standards of conduct described in section eight hundred thirty of this article."

31E-8-826: Court-ordered meeting of directors

31E-8-830, 831, 833: Standards of conduct for directors, Standards of liability for directors, Directors' liability for unlawful distributions

31E-8-840, 841, 842, 843, 844: Required officers, Duties of officers, Standards of conduct for officers, Resignation and removal of officers, Contract right of officers

31E-8-850, 851, 852, 853 (Indemnification) Part definitions, Permissible indemnification, Mandatory indemnification, Advance for expenses

31E-8-854, 855, 856, 857, 858, 859: Circuit court-ordered indemnification and advance for expenses, Determination and authorization of indemnification, Indemnification of officers, Insurance, Variation by corporate action; application of part, Exclusivity of part

31E-8-860: Directors' conflicting interest transactions

31E-10-1001, 1002: Authority to amend, Certain amendments by board of directors

31E-10-1003, 1004, 1005, 1006, 1007, 1008: Amendment by board of directors and members, Amendment by incorporators, Articles of amendment, Restated articles of incorporation, Amendment pursuant to reorganization, Effect of amendment

31E-11-1101, 1102, 1103, 1104: Merger, Action on plan of merger, Articles of merger, Effect of merger

31E-12-1201, 1202: Disposition of assets not requiring member approval, Member approval of certain dispositions

31E-13-1301, 1302, 1303, 1304, 1305: Dissolution by incorporators or initial directors, Dissolution by board of directors and members, Articles of dissolution, Revocation of dissolution, Effect of dissolution

31E-13-1306, 1307: Known claims against dissolved corporation, Unknown claims against dissolved corporation

31E-13-1308, 1309: Adoption of plan for distribution of assets, Liquidating distribution of assets

31E-15-1501, 1502, 1503, 1504, 1505, 1506: Corporate records, Inspection of records by members, Scope of inspection right, Circuit court-ordered inspection, Inspection of records by directors, Exception to notice requirement

"(a) A director of a corporation is entitled to inspect and copy the books, records and documents of the corporation at any reasonable time to the extent reasonably related to the performance of the director's duties as a director, including duties as a member of a committee, but not for any other purpose or in any manner that would violate any duty to the corporation."

31E-15-1520: Financial statement for members

31E-16-1601, 1603: Application to existing domestic corporations, Effective date